Estimating Terrorism Risk

Henry H. Willis, Andrew R. Morral,

Terrence K. Kelly, Jamison Jo Medby

 CENTER FOR TERRORISM RISK MANAGEMENT POLICY

The research described in this report results from the RAND Corporation's continuing program of self-initiated research. Support for such research is provided, in part, by donors and by the independent research and development provisions of RAND's contracts for the operation of its U.S. Department of Defense federally funded research and development centers.

Library of Congress Cataloging-in-Publication Data

Estimating terrorism risk / Henry H. Willis ... [et al.].
    p. cm.
    "MG-388."
    Includes bibliographical references.
    ISBN 0-8330-3834-6 (pbk. : alk. paper)
    1. Terrorism—United States—Prevention. 2. Terrorism—Risk assessment—
United States. 3. Federal aid to terrorism prevention—United States—Planning.
I. Willis, Henry H. II. Rand Corporation.

HV6432.E78 2005
363.32—dc22
                                                   2005024093

Cover photo: Getty Images

The RAND Corporation is a nonprofit research organization providing objective analysis and effective solutions that address the challenges facing the public and private sectors around the world. RAND's publications do not necessarily reflect the opinions of its research clients and sponsors.

RAND® is a registered trademark.

Published 2005 by the RAND Corporation
1776 Main Street, P.O. Box 2138, Santa Monica, CA 90407-2138
1200 South Hayes Street, Arlington, VA 22202-5050
201 North Craig Street, Suite 202, Pittsburgh, PA 15213-1516
RAND URL: http://www.rand.org/
To order RAND documents or to obtain additional information, contact
Distribution Services: Telephone: (310) 451-7002;
Fax: (310) 451-6915; Email: order@rand.org

The RAND Center for Terrorism Risk Management Policy

The RAND Center for Terrorism Risk Management Policy (CTRMP) provides research that is needed to inform public and private decisionmakers on economic security in the face of the threat of terrorism. Terrorism risk insurance studies provide the backbone of the Center's research agenda. Research on the economics of various liability decisions informs the policy decisions of the U.S. Congress and the opinions of state and federal judges. Studies of compensation help Congress to ensure that appropriate compensation is made to the victims of terrorist attacks. Research on security helps to protect critical infrastructure and to improve collective security in rational and cost-effective ways.

CTRMP is housed at the RAND Corporation, an international nonprofit research organization with a reputation for rigorous and objective analysis and the world's leading provider of research on terrorism.

The center combines three organizations:

- RAND Institute for Civil Justice, which brings a 25-year history of empirical research on liability and compensation
- RAND Infrastructure, Safety, and Environment, which conducts research on homeland security and public safety
- Risk Management Solutions, the world's leading provider of models and services for catastrophe risk management.

For additional information about the Center for Terrorism Risk Management Policy, contact:

Robert Reville
RAND Corporation
1776 Main Street
P.O. Box 2138
Santa Monica, CA 90407-2138
Robert_Reville@rand.org
310-393-0411, ext. 6786

Michael Wermuth
RAND Corporation
1200 South Hayes Street
Arlington, VA 22202-5050
Michael_Wermuth@rand.org
703-413-1100, ext. 5414

A profile of the CTRMP, abstracts of its publications, and ordering information can be found at http://www.rand.org/multi/ctrmp.

Center for Terrorism Risk Management Advisory Board

Jeffrey D. DeBoer (co-chair)
President and Chief Executive Officer
Real Estate Roundtable

Jacques Dubois (co-chair)
Chairman
Swiss Re America Holding Corporation

Jack D. Armstrong
Assistant Vice President and Senior
Regulatory Counsel
Liberty Mutual Insurance Company

Kim M. Brunner, Esq.
Executive Vice President and General
Counsel
State Farm Insurance

John Gorte
Executive Vice President
Dorinco/Dow Chemical

Kenneth R. Feinberg, Esq.
Managing Partner
The Feinberg Group, LLP

Ken Jenkins
Senior Vice President, Corporate
Underwriting/Risk Management
American Reinsurance

Bruce Kessler
Executive Vice President and Chief Un-
derwriting Officer
ACE USA

Peter Lowy
Chief Executive Officer
Westfield Corporation, Inc.

Kathleen Nelson
Immediate Past Chair
International Council of Shopping Centers

Art Raschbaum
General Director, Corporate Risk Man-
agement and Insurance
General Motors Corporation

Hemant Shah
President and Chief Executive Officer
Risk Management Solutions, Inc.

Cosette R. Simon
Senior Vice President for Government and
Industry Relations
Swiss Re Life and Health America Inc.

Steven A. Wechsler
President and Chief Executive Officer
NAREIT

Preface

The Department of Homeland Security is responsible for protecting the United States from terrorism through prevention, preparedness, and response. In part, this goal is achieved through allocation of resources to states and urban areas. The Urban Areas Security Initiative (UASI) is a Department of Homeland Security (DHS) grant program designed to enhance security and overall preparedness to prevent, respond to, and recover from acts of terrorism. This program provides financial assistance to address unique planning, equipment, training, and exercise needs of large urban areas (DHS, 2004). Although many stakeholders apparently agree that these allocations should reflect the magnitude of risks to which different areas are exposed, no consensus has emerged on how this might be accomplished.

This monograph examines several challenges to risk-based allocation of homeland security resources. There is not a consistent and shared definition of terrorism risk. Estimating terrorism risk requires treatment of numerous, large uncertainties. There is no existing framework for selecting and combining risk indicators. Finally, little work has been directed toward methods for testing how the accuracy and distribution of risk from different estimates change with respect to a wide range of assumptions about terrorist threats and capabilities and the dearth of information about how security investments might reduce terrorism risk. This monograph addresses each of these issues and proposes solutions to all except the final one, understanding the relationship between investment and risk reduction, which—though a critical problem—has been left for further study.

This research on the general issue of how to estimate terrorism risk is meant to inform resource allocation. It is not a direct assessment of current DHS practice or endorsement of insurance risk modeling. Similarly, it does not represent government policy and is not presented as such. Rather, it is intended to add information and perspective to the rapidly maturing issue of risk-based resource allocation and promote discussion. Further, this monograph presents some data and descriptions of DHS processes from fiscal year 2004 budget planning. The Department's use of risk to inform resource allocations may have since changed, though details of these processes have not been publicly disclosed.

This monograph should be of interest to federal, state, local, and private sector officials responsible for estimating terrorism risks and providing guidance on resource allocation and prioritization based upon these risk estimates.

This study results from the RAND Corporation's continuing program of self-initiated research. Support for such research is provided, in part, by donors and by the independent research and development provisions of RAND's contracts for the operation of its U.S. Department of Defense federally funded research and development centers.

Contents

Figures

Tables

Summary

The Department of Homeland Security (DHS) is responsible for protecting the United States from terrorism through prevention, preparedness, and response. In part, this goal is achieved through allocation of resources to states and urban areas. The Urban Areas Security Initiative (UASI) is a DHS grant program designed to enhance security and overall preparedness by addressing unique planning, equipment, training, and exercise needs of large urban areas (DHS, 2004). Although there appears to be agreement among many stakeholders that these allocations should reflect the magnitude of risks to which different areas are exposed, no consensus has emerged on how this might be accomplished. Indeed, the UASI grant program has frequently been criticized for inadequately calculating risk and therefore for failing to distribute resources in proportion to urban areas' shares of total terrorism risk.

Ultimately, efficient allocation of homeland security resources would be determined based upon assessment of the cost effectiveness of alternative risk-reduction opportunities. After potentially first addressing obvious and easily mitigated risks, this requires understanding the cost effectiveness of different types and amounts of investment. Neither the methods nor the data are available to answer questions about the effectiveness of available risk-reduction alternatives or to determine reasonable minimum standards for community preparedness. Until these questions are answered, allocating homeland security resources based on risk is the next best approach since areas at higher risk are likely to have more and larger opportunities for risk reduction than areas at lower risk. That is, resources would be allocated roughly proportionally to the distribution of risk across areas receiving funding.

This monograph offers a method for constructing an estimate of city risk shares, designed to perform well across a wide range of threat scenarios and risk types. It also proposes and demonstrates a framework for comparing the performance of alternative risk estimates given uncertainty in measuring the elements of risk.

Components of Risk

Terrorism risk can be viewed as having three components: the *threat* to a target, the target's *vulnerability* to the threat, and the *consequences* should the target be successfully attacked. People and organizations represent threats when they have both the intent and capability to damage a target. The *threats* to a target can be measured as the probability that a specific target is attacked in a specific way during a specified period. Thus, a threat might be measured as the annual probability that a city's football stadium will be subject to attack with a radiological weapon.

Vulnerability can be measured as the probability that damage occurs, given a threat. Damages could be fatalities, injuries, property damage, or other consequences; each would have its own vulnerability assessment. *Consequences* are the magnitude and type of damage resulting, given a successful terrorist attack. Risk is a function of all three components: threat, vulnerability, and consequences. These constructs can be used to measure risk consistently in terms of expected annual consequences. More detailed definitions of vulnerability, threat, and risk and discussions of measures for each are presented in this monograph.

Uncertainty and Value Judgments in Terrorism Risk Assessment

There are two important sources of uncertainty in estimating terrorism risk. The first includes variability and error in estimates of threats, vulnerabilities, and consequences. The second involves how we should value different types of consequences. Part of an informed discussion of homeland security policy rests on an understandable and transparent means of accounting for uncertainties in estimates and the consequences of using alternative values.

When facing uncertainty about estimates and values, policy analysis often relies on best estimates, even when they have a low probability of being correct—and a high probability of being wrong. While this allows us to generate a very precise estimate of risk, in the end, if the estimates poorly represent what actually happens in real life, the precision is misplaced. So, rather than seek an optimal method for estimating risk, we seek a method that leads us to make the least egregious errors in decisionmaking across the range of possible scenarios that might develop in the future. Following methods of adaptive planning under deep uncertainty (Davis 1994, 2002; Lempert, Popper, and Bankes, 2003), we seek a method for estimating risk that is robust because it has the lowest expected error when evaluated against a wide range of possible futures.

One approach for developing an estimate with these properties would be first to define multiple sets of threats, vulnerabilities, and consequence measures and use them as the basis for constructing a single risk estimate. Then using these multiple estimates, develop a single description of how risk is distributed that balances across multiple perspectives of terrorism risk.

Generating multiple risk estimates can provide plausible bounds on the magnitude of terrorism risk estimates and how different stakeholders may be affected based on where they live or what outcomes they value most. From several estimates, one can ask how low or high terrorism risk may be in a specific city, what a best estimate of risk is given the range of estimates available, and how answers to these questions differ when considering different types of outcomes. The challenge to analysts defining a single picture of how risk is distributed is to do so without losing significant information. This requires specifying how to deal with the challenges of aggregation given both inherent uncertainties and value choices.

Uncertainty in terrorism risk estimates suggests the need to devise means of hedging our homeland security policies against a range of distributions of risk that are plausible given what we know about uncertainties in our risk estimation procedures. So, rather than seek an optimal method for estimating risk, we seek a method that leads us to make the least egregious errors in decisionmaking across the range of possible scenarios that might develop in the future. This presents a problem comparable to that of forecasting economic trends using multiple estimates or models discussed by Clemen (1989). This literature highlights two objectives to consider when combining estimates: 1) use information contained in the multiple estimates to improve forecasting accuracy and 2) make note of and retain the important distinctions that individual estimates represent.

Addressing multiple values or objectives in terrorism risk estimates differs from combining forecasts. While the goal of combining forecasts is to develop an accurate estimate, the goal of considering multiple objectives is to reflect appropriately the range of values held by stakeholders. Literature on multiobjective decisionmaking provides several approaches for addressing the fact that terrorism risk can be expressed in multiple outcomes. The commonality across these methods is the need to reflect transparently a range of values for multiple objectives in the decisionmaking process.

Simple Versus Complex Risk Indicators

Despite the many sources of uncertainty surrounding terrorism risk, estimating this risk is necessary for informed distribution of homeland security resources. Approaches that have been used in policy analysis for estimating terrorism risk are bounded by two generic categories: simple risk indicators and event-based models. Each approach reflects the components of terrorism risk (i.e., threat, vulnerability, and consequences) and their uncertainties in different ways. As examples of simple indicators, we describe how population and density-weighted population have been used as estimates of terrorism risk. As an example of event-based models, we describe the Risk Management Solutions (RMS) Terrorism Risk Model. These two examples allow for comparisons that illustrate the strengths and weaknesses of each approach.

There is a logical link between population-based indicators and terrorism risk. An argument can be made that consequences are correlated with population and threats are correlated with population density. There are practical benefits for using simple risk indicators such as those based upon population. In general, the metrics for measuring these indicators are well understood and measurable, and data is widely available. The main limitation of these simple indicators is that they do not fully reflect the interactions of threat, vulnerability, and consequences. As a result, there is little consensus and no validated framework for deciding how to use several simple indicators to create a single risk estimator.

Event-based models are built upon relatively detailed analysis of consequences from specific attack scenarios. These models include sensitivity analysis for important parameters that affect consequences. They may include components to model multiple types of events and multiple targets. They may also include modules that translate expert judgments of likelihood or consequences. The strength of event-based models lie in the greater fidelity they enable in analysis. The weakness is that, to obtain this detail, analysts must estimate many uncertain parameters. One example of an event-based model is the RMS Terrorism Risk Model. The RMS model, discussed in more detail later in this monograph, was developed as a tool for the insurance and reinsurance industries to assess risks of macroterrorism.[1]

---

[1] RMS defines *macroterrorism* as attacks capable of causing (1) economic losses in excess of $1 billion, or (2) more than 100 fatalities or 500 injuries, or (3) massively symbolic damage.

Estimating Terrorism Risk

To demonstrate an approach for estimating terrorism risk to inform resource allocations, we calculated a single estimate of U.S. cities' risk shares based on multiple perspectives of terrorism risk obtained from the RMS Terrorism Risk Model. By considering three perspectives on threat (the RMS standard and enhanced and reduced threat outlooks), the RMS results provide three estimates of terrorism risk for the urban areas that received UASI funding in fiscal year 2004. Using these three sets of expected fatalities, we calculated an aggregated risk estimator by minimizing the sum of the squared underestimation error across all urban areas and risk estimates. The assumptions and limitations inherent to this approach are presented in the monograph.

Strengths and Weaknesses of Different Risk Indicators

We compared the proposed aggregated risk estimator to simple population-based indicators, looking at both how the distribution of risk changes for each and the propensity for each to underestimate a city's risk share given the uncertainty that surrounds terrorism risk.

The aggregated risk estimator concentrated most of the expected terrorism losses in relatively few cities compared to population-based indicators. In addition, the aggregated estimator resulted in the lowest underestimates of risk aggregated across all urban areas. Density-weighted population performed better than population alone and was, in fact, quite a bit closer in performance to that of the aggregated indicator than to that of the simple population indicator.

Because the density-weighted population indicator performs well and is easier to derive than the event-based indicator, it might be of utility for some purposes, e.g., in risk-based allocation of resources for strategic purposes over long time intervals, during which relative risk across urban areas is not expected to change much.

Density-weighted population, however, does not allow decisionmakers to see how changes in threat or vulnerability information affect terrorism risk. For example, when making operational resource allocations or evaluating the effectiveness of preparedness programs, decisionmakers need to understand how specific countermeasures reduce or change the profile of terrorism risk. Similarly, a crude indicator like density-weighted population would offer no guidance about how city risk estimates might change with, for instance, new intelligence about terrorist targeting or capabilities of using weapons of mass destruction (WMD). For these purposes, more detailed event-based models of terrorism risk are essential.

In this study, a single event-based estimate was shown to be robust across uncertainties about the likelihood of WMD attacks, uncertainties about which consequences ought to be prioritized in considerations of city risk, and uncertainties about the expected magnitude of risks each city might face. For example, an important observation is that the risk profile of the urban areas examined did not change significantly with the variability of threats from weapons of mass destruction. This is clearly a function of the models used in this study and how they were parameterized. While the primary focus of this study was not to estimate precisely terrorism risk in the United States, this observation raises questions such as whether risk is a characteristic of a region's infrastructure or population that is relatively stable across different threats. If so, this would be an important observation when it comes to policy and resource decisions.

Recommendations

Our framework for defining terrorism risk and the analysis we present here lead us to five recommendations for improving the allocation of homeland security resources:

1. DHS should consistently define terrorism risk in terms of expected annual consequences. Calculating expected annual consequences requires accounting for threat, vulnerability, and consequences. Defining terrorism risk in these terms facilitates the incorporation of risk reduction as the goal of homeland security programs.

2. DHS should seek robust risk estimators that account for uncertainty about terrorism risk and variance in citizen values. Given the tremendous uncertainties surrounding terrorism risk assessment, it is prudent to plan for the range of plausible futures that may play out. Several approaches are available for generating estimates of city risk shares that offer robust characterizations of risk across multiple uncertainties and perspectives on relative values of different consequences. Our approach to this problem ensures that underestimation error is minimized.

3. DHS should develop event-based models of terrorism risk, like that demonstrated in this monograph. Measuring and tracking levels of terrorism risk is an important component of homeland security policy. These data provide insight into how current programs are reducing risk and when and where new terrorist threats may be emerging. Only event-based models of terrorism risk provide insight into how changes in assumptions or actual levels of threat, vulnerability, and consequences affect risk levels.

4. Until reliable event-based models are constructed, density-weighted population should be preferred over population as a simple risk indicator. Density-weighted population is reasonably correlated with the distribution of terrorism risk across the United States, as estimated by event-based models like the RMS Terrorism Risk Model. To support strategic policy decisions when the effects of new countermeasures or recent intelligence are not in question, density-weighted population is a useful indicator in lieu of event-based models. In contrast, our results suggest that population offers a remarkably weak indicator of risk, not much superior to estimating risk shares at random.

5. DHS should fund research to bridge the gap between terrorism risk assessment and resource allocation policies that are cost effective. We do not here seek to understand how UASI allocation amounts may reduce risk. Until that relationship is understood, resource allocation decisions will not be optimized for reducing casualties and property loss. To these ends, DHS should evaluate the performance of the formula used to assign UASI grants using the approach presented in this study.

Acknowledgments

We would like to thank our RAND colleagues who provided guidance, comments, and spirited debate during this project. These include Jim Bonomo, Paul Davis, Brian Jackson, Tom LaTourrette, Rob Lempert, Martin Libicki, Steven Popper, Jack Riley, Russ Shaver, and Mike Wermuth. We were supported through valuable collaboration and review by Risk Management Solutions, Inc. (RMS), with regard to the RMS Terrorism Risk Model, specifically by Derek Blum, Andrew Coburn, Alie Cohen, and Arlene Kim Suda. The project also benefited from insightful informal reviews through the board of the RAND Center for Terrorism Risk Management Policy, which is codirected by Bob Reville and Jack Riley. Finally, we appreciated the thorough formal reviews of the draft manuscript by Bruce Don, Yacov Haimes, and Darius Lakdawalla.

While our work has benefited greatly from interactions with colleagues, collaborators, and reviewers, the views presented in this monograph are, of course, our own responsibility.

Glossary

CBRN	chemical, biological, radiological, or nuclear
CTRMP	Center for Terrorism Risk Management Policy
DHS	Department of Homeland Security
E[X]	expected value of X
LNG	liquefied natural gas
P(X)	probability that event X will occur
P(X|Y)	probability that event X will occur, given that event Y already has occurred
RMS	Risk Management Solutions
TNT	trinitrotoluene
TRIA	Terrorism Risk Insurance Act of 2002
UASI	Urban Areas Security Initiative
U.S.	United States
WMD	weapons of mass destruction

CHAPTER ONE

Introduction

The Urban Areas Security Initiative (UASI) is a Department of Homeland Security (DHS) grant program designed to enhance security and overall preparedness to prevent, respond to, and recover from acts of terrorism. These goals are accomplished by providing financial assistance to address the unique planning, equipment, training, and exercise needs of large urban areas (DHS, 2004).

In fiscal year 2004, UASI provided $675 million to 50 urban areas perceived to be at highest risk from terrorist attacks. These funds were allocated using a formula that accounted for several indicators of the terrorism risk to which each urban area might be exposed. Though precise details of the formula are not publicly available, it reportedly calculates each urban area's share of total terrorism risk based on city population, infrastructure, and threat information, giving indicators for each factor an importance weight of nine, six, and three, respectively. Despite this effort to allocate homeland security resources based on the relative risks to which each urban area is exposed, the Department of Homeland Security has frequently been criticized for inadequately calculating risk and therefore for failing to distribute resources in proportion to urban areas' shares of total terrorism risk (U.S. House of Representatives, 2003).

Debates about the proper allocation of resources have suffered from several problems. For instance, currently, there is no shared and precise definition of terrorism risk, so stakeholders in the debate are often referring to different concepts of risk. Even if a precise definition were widely used, there are no standard methods for estimating and monitoring changes in the level and nature of terrorism risks. Instead, various indicators of risk have been used (for instance in the UASI formula) or proposed (e.g., Canada, 2003), which are presumed to correspond in some way with true terrorism risk. To our knowledge, however, no systematic frameworks for selecting these indicators or aggregating them into a unitary measure of risk are yet available. Moreover, terrorism risk changes over time as terrorist motives, capabilities, and targets change and adapt to risk-mitigation efforts. These facts defy the efficacy of any simplistic model that attempts to enumerate a single index as a measure of risk. Measuring terrorism risk must always reflect uncertainties in estimates of the relative risks faced by different cities.

Risk Assessment Versus Resource Allocation

Ultimately, efficient allocation of homeland security resources would be determined based upon assessment of the cost effectiveness of alternative risk-reduction opportunities. This requires understanding the cost effectiveness of different types and amounts of investment. As a hypothetical example, even if terrorism risks were greater in New York City than in Des Moines, Iowa, allocating resources according to proportion of risk would not be optimal if available countermeasures are more cost effective in Des Moines.[1] For example, terrorists could respond strategically to countermeasures in New York City and target less-protected areas, or the marginal effectiveness of resources spent in New York City may decrease with continuing investment. Neither the methods nor the data are available to answer questions about the effectiveness of available risk-reduction alternatives or to determine reasonable minimum standards for community preparedness. Until these questions are answered, allocating homeland security resources based on risk is the next best approach since areas at higher risk are likely to have more and larger opportunities for risk reduction

---

sions of how terrorist strategy affects resource allocation decisionmaking, see , 2002b) and Lakdawalla and Zanjani (2004).

than are areas at lower risk. That is, resources would b
roughly proportionally to the distribution of risk across a
ing funding.

There are several other reasons why it is still importan. ₁ur decisionmakers to understand the levels and distribution of terrorism risk.
First, because assessing risk and risk reduction is a critical first step in
assessing cost effectiveness of counterterrorism efforts, methods developed to support terrorism risk assessment will also support analysis
of resource allocation. Further, even when large risks are not mitigated by current efforts, identifying them can help direct intelligence
gathering, research, and future counterterrorism efforts. Finally, following changes in the levels and patterns of terrorism risk over time
provides insights into the effectiveness of current efforts and the
emergence of new risks.

Scope and Limitations

In this monograph, we propose a specific definition of terrorism risk
that can be operationalized for practical problems facing DHS and
develop a method of constructing a single measure of risk that accounts for uncertainties in risk measurement. We then propose and
demonstrate a framework for evaluating this measure, along with alternative measures of risk, to understand resulting errors given uncertainties in their measurement. Finally, we offer recommendations on
future efforts to calculate the shares of total terrorism risk to which
different areas are exposed.

While the discussions in this monograph focus on a specific
program, the UASI grants, the problems discussed previously are
common to a number of risk estimation problems in homeland security. Thus, the problem is a general one of decisionmaking under uncertainty, and the solutions presented here are also generalizable to
similar decision contexts.

This monograph does not address all problems identified previously. This treatment of risk estimation does not fully inform specification of a formula for risk-based allocation of homeland security re-

sources. As noted previously, before such a formula can be constructed, additional research is needed to understand the relationship between resource allocation and risk reduction.

The scope of this project is further limited to the direct consequences associated with terrorism threats. Thus, we do not include in our estimates of terrorism risk the secondary and higher order economic or other losses that result from an attack on a given location. These effects are important and may well constitute the major portion of the risk but can be handled by the methods we develop here given additional resources. Such analysis would extend this current work to further improve the evaluation of the relative risks to which different urban areas are exposed and thus would help to improve the allocation of homeland security resources.

Overview of This Monograph

The remainder of this monograph is organized as follows. Chapter Two defines terrorism risk and the factors it comprises. Chapter Three discusses the sources of uncertainty that must be addressed when incorporating terrorism risk assessment into policy decision-making and provides guidance on how each form of uncertainty can be addressed. In Chapter Four, we discuss alternative approaches to estimating levels of terrorism risk across UASI-funded urban areas and propose a method for combining diverse risk estimates into a single estimate of each urban area's share of total terrorism risk. In Chapter Five, we develop a framework for evaluating the performance of different risk estimators given uncertainties about the distribution of true terrorism risk and the diversity of types of consequences that must be considered. Finally, we discuss the performance of the alternative risk estimators and the implications our findings have for homeland security policy.

CHAPTER TWO

Terrorism Risk and Its Components

Differing notions of terrorism risk frequently fuel disagreements about the relative risks to which different regions or cities are exposed. Some arguments implicitly link risk to terrorism threats. If, for example, one city were known through gathered intelligence or past history to be the preferred target for terrorists, this view would support a claim that this city has a high level of terrorism risk. Alternatively, others argue that risk is more closely associated with infrastructure vulnerabilities within a region because these represent logical targets for terrorism. Thus, for example, even if we do not know of a threat to a nuclear power plant, reason and prudence argue that we should include that facility in considering a region's risk. Finally, discussions of risk occasionally emphasize the possible consequences of terrorist attacks in evaluating risk. Thus, if two cities have similar chemical storage facilities, but one has the facility located close to its population center, a persuasive argument can be made that the nearer-to-population city's chemical facility presents a greater risk than the other city's.

Clearly, strong arguments can be made that threats, vulnerabilities, and consequences play a significant part in the overall risk to which a city is exposed. What has been less clear is how these three components are related. In this chapter, we offer a definition of risk that links them. We also distinguish between definitions for threat, vulnerability, consequences, and risks and the measures that can be used to assess and track each.

Threat

People or organizations represent a terrorist threat when they have the intent and capability to impose damage to a target. Note that neither intentions without capabilities nor capabilities without intentions pose a threat. Threat only exists when both are manifested together in a person or organization. Allocating homeland security resources to protect critical infrastructure or cities requires measuring the threats posed to specific targets or from specific types of attack. When the scope of threat is defined in terms of a specific set of targets, a specific set of attack types, and a specific time period, probability can be used as a measure of the likelihood that an attack will occur. Thus, we define a measure of threat as follows:

Measure (Threat): *The probability that a specific target is attacked in a specific way during a specified time period, or*

$$\text{Threat} = P(\text{attack occurs})$$

This measure of terrorist threat emphasizes a specific type of attack on specific targets. Radiological attack represents a different threat to a specific target than nuclear attack. Attacks on stadiums represent different threats than attacks on skyscrapers. A complete description of the threats to which a target is exposed would require consideration of every mode of attack separately. In practice, however, it may suffice to focus on a limited number of attack types that are representative of chemical, biological, radiological, or nuclear (CBRN) and explosive attack modes. Similarly, it may suffice to focus on a limited number of target types or groups of targets in a region.

This measure of threat is specified in terms of attack types and targets. The intelligence community more customarily considers threat in terms of groups of attackers given its interest identifying and stopping those who might pose a threat. An attack-type perspective is more useful for the task of resource allocation because the decision context is most concerned with what targets are threatened than with by whom and why.

Finally, since our measure for threat is uncertain, one should keep in mind that it can also be represented by a probability distribution, not a point estimate. These definitions are consistent with methods and terminology proposed through applications of engineering risk analysis to terrorism risk assessment (Ayyub, 2005; Paté-Cornell, 2005; von Winterfeldt and Rosoff, 2005).

Vulnerability

Clearly, not all threats of the same type are equally important. Furthermore, the threat of terrorism is dynamic in that it adapts to current conditions that affect the likelihood of attack success. For example, even if a typical hotel and fortified military base have equal probability of being subjected to a car-bomb attack, the attack would be more likely to achieve the aim of causing significant damage at the less-secure hotel. Therefore, we also need a precise definition of vulnerability that captures information about the infrastructure in which we are interested.

Paraphrasing Haimes, *vulnerability is the manifestation of the inherent states of the system (e.g., physical, technical, organizational, cultural) that can result in damage if attacked by an adversary.*[1] Referring again to the domain of engineering risk analysis, where threat can be thought of as being a load or force acting on a system, vulnerability can be thought of as being the capacity of a system to respond to this threat (Paté-Cornell, 2005). To use this definition for measurement, we must be more specific and ask, "vulnerable to what?" Probability can be used as a measure of the likelihood that vulnerability will lead to damage when attacks occur.

---

[1] Haimes (2004, p. 699). We note that most of this italicized phrase is verbatim from this source, but we have changed the definition slightly so as not to imply that an attacker needs to exploit a vulnerability knowingly—that is, a target can be vulnerable without the vulnerability being recognized by an attacker.

Measure (Vulnerability): *The probability that damages (where damages may involve fatalities, injuries, property damage, or other consequences) occur, given a specific attack type, at a specific time, on a given target, or*

$$\text{Vulnerability} = P(\text{attack results in damage} \mid \text{attack occurs})$$

In other words, a target's vulnerability can be articulated as the probability that an attack of a given type will be successful once it has been launched and, as articulated, measures vulnerability to specific types of damages only (i.e., there would be separate vulnerability assessments for deaths, injuries, and property damage).

Note that for the measure specified above, magnitude of the damage is not part of the definition of vulnerability. This measure assumes a simplified representation of vulnerability in which there is either a successful attack with damage or no success with no damage. As a result, we define "success" in terms of whether or not damage, having a distribution of magnitude, is inflicted by the attack. Consequence measurement is discussed below. A more general model (used in many military analyses) is that there is a range of damage levels, each associated with its own probability. This is simply a more discrete representation of damage and defense mechanisms.

Consequences

We define "consequence" as the magnitude and type of damage resulting from successful terrorist attacks. To define a measure of consequence, specificity is again required. In this case, specificity requires treatment of two important considerations: how consequences are measured and how uncertainty is addressed. Formally, we state this as follows:

Measure (Consequence): *The expected magnitude of damage (e.g., deaths, injuries, or property damage), given a specific attack type, at a specific time, that results in damage to a specific target or,*

$$\text{Consequence} = E(\text{damage} \mid \text{attack occurs and results in damage})$$

Consequences can be expressed in terms of fatalities, injuries, economic losses, or other types of damage. Other aspects of consequences can also be considered using the approach we outline here and this definition. For example, the damage or destruction of critical infrastructures that cause injury, loss of life, and economic damage outside the area of immediate attack are important. They may in fact dominate the results of an analysis if the impact on society as a whole is considered rather than the impact on the target and its occupants and owners.[2] In this monograph, however, we limit our focus to mortality, morbidity, and economic loss at the point of attack in order to illustrate an approach to risk estimation in a manner that is transparent yet relevant to real-world policy decisions.

As discussed in detail in Chapter Three, consequences are determined by many uncertain factors, such as wind speed or relative humidity (which could be important factors in a chemical or biological attack, for example). These uncertainties can be addressed by considering a full distribution for potential consequences or specific points along this distribution. Haimes (2004) notes that risk assessment of rare and extreme events requires special consideration of the tails of these distributions, and that the expected value often misrepresents true risk. Conversely, estimates of the tail of the distribution will be very dependent upon assumptions when considering events like terrorism where there is great uncertainty about events and limited historical information. For this reason, and to simplify, our continued discussion of consequences considers the expected value of the distribution of damage.

---

[2] See Rinaldi, Peerenboom, and Kelly (2001) for a comprehensive discussion of these topics.

Risk as a Function of Threat, Vulnerability, and Consequences

Risk is the anticipated consequences over some period of time to a defined set of targets, resulting from a defined set of threats. For a specific threat, target, and type of consequence, risk can be measured as follows:

Measure (Terrorism Risk): *The expected consequence of an existent threat, which for a given target, attack mode, and damage type can be expressed as*

$$\text{Risk} = P(\text{attack occurs})$$
$$* \, P(\text{attack results in damage} \, | \, \text{attack occurs})$$
$$* \, E(\text{damage} \, | \, \text{attack occurs and results in damage})$$
$$= \text{Threat} * \text{Vulnerability} * \text{Consequence}$$

In other words, terrorism risk represents the expected consequences of attacks taking into account the likelihood that attacks occur and that they are successful if attempted. In probabilistic terms, risk from an attack of a certain type is the unconditional expected value of damages of a certain type.

There are two advantages of using this formulation of terrorism risk. First, it provides an approach for comparing and aggregating terrorism risk. With this definition, it is possible to compare risks of a specific type across diverse targets such as airports and electrical substations. For example, the injury risk from an explosives attack could be expressed for both as the expected annual injuries resulting from such attacks against each target. Estimating overall terrorism risk requires further analysis that considers all threat types and targets. If risks were independent, expected damages of a specific type could be aggregated by summing across threat types and target types.[3] However, dependencies likely exist between risks. For instance, a successful nuclear attack in a city could dramatically change the expected risks for targets in the damage footprint of the explosion.

Second, this definition of risk provides a clear mapping between risk and approaches to managing or reducing risk. Intelligence and active defense involving "taking the fight to the enemy" represent an approach to risk management that focuses specifically on threats. Managing risk through vulnerability requires increasing surveillance and detection, hardening targets, or other capabilities that might reduce the success of attempted attacks. Finally, risk can be managed through consequences by increasing preparedness and response that reduces the effects of damage through mitigation or compensation.

---

[3] Damage of different types (i.e., casualties versus economic damages) should be treated using approaches of multiobjective decisionmaking, not simple aggregation. This is discussed further in Chapter Three.

Accounting for Uncertainty and Values in Terrorism Risk Assessment

The definitions and measures presented in Chapter Two provide a simplified perspective on threat, vulnerability, consequences, and risk that is useful for thinking about homeland security and preparedness. The reality that threat, vulnerability, and consequences are all subject to tremendous uncertainties makes estimating each a challenging task. To facilitate risk estimation, it is important to understand the sources of these uncertainties that affect terrorism risk.

There are two important sources of uncertainty in estimating terrorism risk. The first includes variability and error in estimates of threats, vulnerabilities, and consequences. For example, exact knowledge of the threat would require comprehensive intelligence on the plans and capabilities of all terrorist groups. Since this level of precision is not feasible, expert judgments must be substituted for fact, resulting in parameter estimates for threats that are subject to uncertainty or frank disagreements.

The second source of uncertainty concerns how we should value different types of consequences. This is a fundamental problem underlying homeland security decisions that inevitably share burdens of cost and risk among different parts of U.S. society. For instance, if a city has a small property-loss risk, but a large fatality risk, you might conclude that it has medium overall terrorism risk by valuing the importance of each type of consequence as roughly equivalent. In fact, any strategy for judging the relative importance of different types of consequence represents an attempt to estimate the value that we (society or the United States) should or does place on each consequence.

Because this requires value judgments—and potentially contentious ones—it must ultimately be discussed by the public and policymakers. Part of an informed discussion of this judgment rests on an understandable and transparent illustration of the consequences of using alternative values.

Uncertainties in the Estimation of Threat, Vulnerability, and Consequences

At any moment, we may assume that a target has exact, true values for threat, vulnerability, consequences and therefore for risk. These values, however, cannot be directly observed, so must be estimated. Estimation introduces uncertainty and error.

Probably the greatest source of uncertainty derives from estimates of threat, which concerns terrorists' goals, motives, and capabilities. Our sources of information on these factors—chiefly intelligence, historical analysis, and expert judgment—support only crude estimates of the probability of attacks against specific targets or classes of targets (e.g., banks). Experts frequently disagree about the goals of terrorist groups and their capabilities, and some terror groups may exist about which little is known. Consequently, assessments of terrorist motivations and capabilities may systematically under- or overestimate threats. Given this, our threat estimates must be treated with suspicion.

Vulnerability estimates may be subject to lower levels of uncertainty. Because vulnerability concerns the likelihood that an attack of a specific type and magnitude will be successful against a target, it concerns matters that can, in principle, be carefully studied and for which rough estimates may be reasonably good, e.g., the methods of engineering risk analysis that have been used successfully in estimating risks of space flight and operating nuclear reactors. These methods can be applied to protecting targets and infrastructure (Haimes, 2004). Despite the applicability of such approaches, imprecision remains in the estimation of a target's vulnerability.

The sources of uncertainty in consequences concern damage assessments that depend on the physical situation at the target when the attack occurs. For example, suppose a chemical weapon that takes the form of a spray of fine droplets is used at a popular oceanfront recreational location on a busy weekend afternoon and that the chemicals are only effective while they remain in droplet form—that is, they are not effective after they evaporate. If the atmospheric conditions are hot and dry, and the wind is blowing from the land out over the sea, then the droplets might evaporate more quickly due to the dry heat and will blow out over the water away from areas where many people gather. However, if the weather conditions are such that the wind is blowing over the beach on a humid day, the damage from fatalities and injuries might be more severe.

This example illustrates that estimating consequences requires a substantial amount of work. Fortunately, this work is often in the form of straightforward engineering and statistical problems, and well-developed models exist of many natural disasters that are directly applicable, or nearly so. Additionally, the military and other government agencies have long studied the effects of weapons on people and structures, and this, too, is useful for estimating consequences. For example, modeling has been used to estimate the consequences of attacks such as releases of hazardous chemicals or biological agents, radiological bombs, conventional explosions, and nuclear detonations (Abt, 2003; Bozette et al., 2003; RMS, 2003). Other approaches, like the Interoperability Input-Output model (Haimes, 2004), use economic data to understand the indirect economic consequences of attacks resulting from interdependence between market sectors. Although more information is available on many consequences, the precision with which that information may be applied should not be overstated. The RMS Terrorism Risk Model described in Chapter Four is built upon thousands of estimates from these types of detailed models. Applying detailed event models requires estimation of numerous parameters, a process that itself introduces uncertainty.

Reflecting Values in Terrorism Risk Management

Models of terrorist attacks can assess impacts in terms of injuries and fatalities, property loss, economic losses, citizen confidence and feelings of security, or myriad other potentially relevant outcomes. Risk can likewise be expressed in terms of any one, or a combination, of these consequences.

The emphasis placed on each type of consequence in the evaluation of terrorism risk is a value judgment. While all types of risk could mathematically be combined into a single-dimensional aggregate risk, any such aggregation requires making value judgments on the relative importance of different consequences. This multidimensional nature of consequences creates difficult decisions for policymakers who must weigh the relative importance of different types of consequences when allocating homeland security resources.

As an example, consider two regions. The first, a densely populated business district, may be viewed as a terrorist target for being a hub of economic activity. Terrorist attacks at this location could produce large numbers of fatalities and vast economic losses. The second region, an industrial park where petroleum refining and transferring take place, could also be considered a target. For this case, economic losses may be equally large; however, because of lower population densities, expected fatalities might be lower.

The priorities given to these two regions in estimating risk are driven by values—in other words, the relative weight assigned to a particular type of consequences. Different stakeholder groups will have different perspectives. Some may believe that mitigating risk is exclusively about the prevention of deaths and injuries, and thus the business district bears the greatest burden of risk. Another group may value minimizing damage to the domestic economy more, and consequently believe that risk is divided more equally between the two regions. In our system of allocating homeland security resources, decisionmakers have an important role in understanding and representing diverse sets of values. In the end, the approach used in the decisionmaking process should allow transparency, so that citizens can effectively participate in risk-management deliberations (Stern and Fineberg, 1996).

Implications of Uncertainty and Values for Managing Terrorism Risk

The uncertainties described earlier ensure there will be disagreement on how to model terrorist events and protection strategies, how to specify probability distributions to represent threat or vulnerability, and how to value diverse measures of consequences. Lempert, Popper, and Bankes (2003) define these conditions as reflecting a state of deep uncertainty. Deep uncertainty has important implications for decisionmakers charged with developing policies that depend on terrorism risk assessments, like risk-based allocation formulae.

Often policy analysis relies on best estimates even when they have a low probability of being correct—and a high probability of being wrong. While this generates a very precise estimate of risk, in the end, if the estimates poorly represent what actually happens in real life, the precision is misplaced. Lempert, Popper, and Bankes (2003) propose an alterative approach when addressing conditions of deep uncertainty. The approach specifies a wide range of future scenarios that could unfold and then challenges decisionmakers to choose strategies that perform well across a large number of these possible futures, rather than for a single best estimate of the future. This approach is consistent with methods of capabilities-based planning that the Department of Defense has adopted to ensure adaptiveness in response to uncertainty about future threats (Davis, 1994, 2002).

By analogy, if we believed some model of the stock market was very reliable or subject to low rates of error, then we would allocate most or all of our investment in those stocks it predicts to rise. That is, we would base our policy chiefly on the model's best estimates. In contrast, if we believed the same estimates were subject to considerable error, we would be wise to hedge our investments against alternative possible market outcomes within the range of plausible futures suggested by the uncertainty around our model estimates. Similarly, in this chapter, we argue that uncertainty in terrorism risk estimates suggests the need to devise means of hedging our homeland security policies against a range of distributions of risk that are plausible given what we know about uncertainties in our risk-estimation procedures.

So, rather than seek an optimal method for estimating risk, we seek a method that leads us to make the least egregious errors in decisionmaking across the range of possible scenarios that might develop in the future. In other words, following Lempert, Popper, and Bankes (2003), when confronting deep uncertainty we seek a method for estimating risk that is robust because it has the lowest expected error when evaluated against a wide range of possible futures. This decision rule is conceptually similar to Savage's minimax principle and regret minimization (Savage, 1951).

One approach for developing an estimate with these properties would be first to define multiple sets of threats, vulnerabilities, and consequence measures and use them as the basis for constructing a single risk estimate. Then, using these multiple estimates, one could develop a single description of how risk is distributed that balances across multiple perspectives of terrorism risk. This estimate would describe the distribution of aggregate risk and would potentially be robust across a wide range of possible futures and values. That is, an estimate may be designed to minimize the error between estimated risk and actual risks that may materialize as the future unfolds.

Each estimate of threats, vulnerabilities, and consequences represents a different view of what is valued and likely to take place in the future. These views could be results from multiple parameterizations of a single model, results from multiple models, or the perspectives of different experts. The different views could produce estimates of the concentration of terrorism risk in different geographic areas, through different modes of attack, or for different types of consequences. For example, in each view, a different region might be found to have the greatest share of terrorism risk, or consequences may be measured using a different outcome.

Generating multiple risk estimates provides information about the bounds of understanding about terrorism risk and how different stakeholders may be affected based on where they live or what outcomes they value most. From several estimates, one can ask how low or high terrorism risk may be in a specific city, what a best estimate of risk is given the range of estimates available, and how answers to these questions differ when considering different types of outcomes. The challenge to analysts defining a single picture of how risk is distributed is to do so without losing significant information. This requires specifying how to deal with the challenges of aggregation given both inherent uncertainties and value choices discussed previously.

Aggregating Risk Estimates

The previous discussion suggests that uncertainty in terrorism risk estimates can be addressed through simple aggregations of multiple perspectives on threat. In fact, this approach has proved useful in another field, economic forecasting. Combining economic forecasts is conceptually similar to combining estimates of terrorism risk. In each case, there is uncertainty about future events that increases as one focuses further into the future. For both terrorism and economic forecasting, competing models exist built on different assumptions about model structure and parameters. In several cases, the competing models for each are highly correlated. Clemen's (1989) literature review demonstrates that combining economic forecasts can improve the accuracy of predictions and that simple aggregations of estimates, such as averaging, can perform well when compared to more complex methods that take into account correlations between estimates or judgments of forecast quality. Of course, the hazard of aggregating forecasts is that important divergent perspectives might be lost. For example, Morgan and Keith (1995) demonstrated that expert judgments about climate change reveal tremendous diversity of opinion. Thus, it is important to achieve two goals when combining forecasts: 1) achieving the potential gains in accuracy that come from multiple forecasts and 2) make note of and retain the important distinctions that individual forecasts represent.

Values and Multiobjective Decisionmaking

Addressing multiple values or objectives in terrorism risk estimates differs from combining forecasts. While the goal of combining forecasts is to develop an accurate estimate, the goal of considering multiple objectives is to reflect appropriately the range of values held by stakeholders. For example, a terrorism risk estimation model may yield estimated losses in terms of fatalities and economic damage. Using the estimate of fatalities is not more accurate or inaccurate than using the estimate of economic damages. Rather, it is important that decisionmakers understand and consider the tradeoffs across consequence types (or objectives) when selecting among policy alternatives.

Literature on multiobjective decisionmaking provides several approaches for addressing the fact that terrorism risk can be expressed in multiple outcomes. Methods such as multiattribute utility analysis (Keeney and Raiffa, 1993) and multiobjective value models (Keeney, 1992) emphasize the need to structure decisions, elicit stakeholder preferences, and apply axiomatic rules for combining outcomes. Tradeoff analysis (Hammond, Keeney, and Raiffa, 1999; Chankong and Haimes, 1983) reduces the burden of the elicitation process by identifying dominating alternatives and eliminating inferior choices through specification of equivalent choices across objectives. Hierarchical Holographic Modeling incorporates multiple objectives by capturing and representing alternative views of a given problem for decisionmakers (Haimes, 2004). The commonality across these methods is the need to reflect transparently a range of values for multiple objectives in the decisionmaking process.

Though multiobjective decisionmaking is an essential part of the policy process, the remainder of this monograph provides a demonstration of different approaches to estimating risk and combining estimates without attempting to characterize stakeholders' values or preferences. Instead, we only discuss risk in terms of expected fatalities. Thus, to the extent that risks are distributed differently if measured as injuries or economic consequences, this becomes an additional source of uncertainty in our estimation of overall risk. A comprehensive terrorism risk assessment must allow decisionmakers to understand the implications of different value judgments. Thus, estimates presented in subsequent chapters of this monograph must be interpreted with this limitation in mind.

CHAPTER FOUR

Two Approaches to Estimating Terrorism Risk in Urban Areas

Despite the many sources of uncertainty surrounding terrorism risk, estimating this risk is necessary for informed distribution of homeland security resources. This chapter describes two approaches for estimating terrorism risk: simple risk indicators and event-based models. Each approach reflects the components of terrorism risk (i.e., threat, vulnerability, and consequences) and their uncertainties in different ways. As examples of simple indicators, we describe how population and density-weighted population have been used as estimates of terrorism risk. As an example of event-based models, we describe the RMS Terrorism Risk Model. These two examples allow for comparisons that illustrate each approach's strengths and weaknesses.

Simple Risk Indicators: Population-Based Metrics

Population is often incorporated into simple indicators of terrorism risk. The DHS State Homeland Security Grant Program uses a combination of equal allocation of resources and use of population as a simple proxy for terrorism risk. In its first several years of funding, the program allocated its first cut of funding so that each state received 0.75 percent of the total resources. The second cut allocated the remaining funding in proportion to each state's population (Ransdell and Booorian, 2004). Proposed legislation would reduce the guaranteed amount directed to each state and require that the remaining funds are allocated with consideration of threat. The UASI grant program allocation formula, mentioned previously, is also partially based on population.

There is a logical link between population-based indicators and terrorism risk. An argument can be made that consequences are correlated with population. However, terrorism risks to a population of 100,000 are clearly different if that population resides in a dense urban area rather than if it is spread across a larger rural area because of the higher probability of many high-profile targets and more people within any given attack footprint. Density-weighted population, i.e., the product of a region's population and its population density, offers one of many possible simple risk indicators that account for this difference. Just as population can be considered correlated with consequences, so too is population density correlated with threat. For example, a terrorist targeting 1,000 people might be more likely to attack a group when they are all within the same city block than if they are dispersed across the country. In evaluating alternative approaches for allocating resources, the Congressional Research Service noted that population and density-weighted population are correlated though result in different distributions of resources (Canada 2003). There are practical benefits for using simple risk indicators such as those based upon population. In general, the metrics for measuring these indicators are well understood, measurable, and data is widely available. For example, the 2000 U.S. Census is a very credible source for data on the population and population density for the UASI-funded urban areas. Table 4.1 shows this data along with the funding each area received in FY2004.

Table 4.1
Population, Population Density, Density-Weighted Population, and Grant
Allocations for Urban Areas Receiving UASI Funding in Fiscal Year 2004

Urban Areas	Population[a]	Population Density[a] (per Square Mile)	Density-Weighted Population[b]	FY2004 UASI Grant Allocation[c] ($ million)
Albany-Schenectady-Troy	875,583	272	237,926,588	7
Atlanta	4,112,198	672	2,761,386,037	11
Baltimore	2,552,994	979	2,498,144,264	16
Baton Rouge	602,894	380	229,154,762	7
Boston, MA-NH	3,406,829	1,685	5,740,709,241	19
Buffalo-Niagara Falls	1,170,111	747	873,657,856	10
Charlotte-Gastonia-Rock Hill, NC-SC	1,499,293	444	665,682,378	7
Chicago	8,272,768	1,634	13,519,096,414	34
Cincinnati, OH-KY-IN	1,646,395	493	811,141,960	13
Cleveland-Lorain-Elyria	2,250,871	832	1,871,707,337	10
Columbus, OH	1,540,157	490	755,141,752	9
Dallas	3,519,176	569	2,002,093,120	12
Denver	2,109,282	561	1,183,064,989	9
Detroit	4,441,551	1,140	5,062,484,593	14
Fresno	922,516	114	105,084,482	7
Houston	4,177,646	706	2,948,039,040	20
Indianapolis	1,607,486	456	733,470,541	10
Jersey City	608,975	13,044	7,943,237,618	17
Kansas City, MO-KS	1,776,062	329	583,476,273	13
Las Vegas, NV-AZ	1,563,282	40	62,076,079	11
Los Angeles-Long Beach[d]	9,519,338	2,344	22,314,867,674	40
Louisville, KY-IN	1,025,598	495	507,651,616	9
Memphis, TN-AR-MS	1,135,614	378	428,953,952	10
Miami, FL	2,253,362	1,158	2,609,185,020	19
Milwaukee-Waukesha, WI	1,500,741	1,028	1,542,728,464	10
Minneapolis-St. Paul, MN-WI[e]	2,968,806	490	1,453,687,745	20
New Haven-Meriden, CT	542,149	1,261	683,670,545	10
New Orleans	1,337,726	394	526,405,217	7

Table 4.1—continued

Urban Areas	Population[a]	Population Density[a] (per Square Mile)	Density-Weighted Population[b]	FY2004 UASI Grant Allocation[c] ($ million)
New York, NY	9,314,235	8,159	75,991,762,554	47
Newark, NJ	2,032,989	1,289	2,619,713,383	15
Oakland, CA	2,392,557	1,642	3,927,449,645	8
Orange County, CA[f]	2,846,289	3,606	10,262,626,470	25
Orlando	1,644,561	471	774,794,778	9
Philadelphia, PA-NJ	5,100,931	1,323	6,749,136,215	23
Phoenix-Mesa	3,251,876	223	725,649,640	12
Pittsburgh	2,358,695	510	1,202,742,683	12
Portland-Vancouver, OR-WA	1,918,009	381	731,703,925	8
Richmond-Petersburg	996,512	338	337,254,906	7
Sacramento	1,628,197	399	649,623,296	8
St. Louis, MO-IL	2,603,607	407	1,060,496,877	11
San Antonio	1,592,383	479	762,291,362	6
San Diego	2,813,833	670	1,885,205,299	10
San Francisco	1,731,183	1,705	2,951,064,038	26
San Jose	1,682,585	1,304	2,193,476,169	10
Seattle-Bellevue-Everett	2,414,616	546	1,318,032,823	17
Tampa-St. Petersburg-Clearwater	2,395,997	938	2,247,784,596	9
Washington, DC-MD-VA-WV	4,923,153	756	3,723,526,125	29

NOTES: (a) Data from U.S. Census Bureau (2000). (b) Calculated as population^2/mile^2. (c) Data from DHS (2004) rounded to the nearest $ million. (d) Los Angeles and Long Beach received separate UASI disbursements though are considered together in this analysis. (e) Minneapolis and St. Paul received separate UASI disbursements though are considered together in this analysis. (f) Santa Ana and Anaheim received separate UASI disbursement though are considered together in this analysis as Orange County.

However, there are limitations to using simple indicators of terrorism risk. The main limitation is that they do not fully reflect the interactions of threat, vulnerability, or consequences discussed in Chapter Two. As a result, there is little consensus and no validated framework for deciding how to use several simple indicators to create a single risk estimator. For example, one simple indicator of risk with respect to biological attacks on livestock might be the size of the live-stock population. However, there is no theoretical or empirical basis for deciding whether counts of livestock should be included as an agroterrorism indicator in a model of a region's overall risk, and if so, in what proportion to other indicators like population or energy in-frastructure. Furthermore, including an indicator like livestock could dramatically alter conclusions about the distribution of risk across regions. In short, therefore, stakeholders with concerns about differ-ent types of terrorism are unlikely to agree upon any model of risk that relies on a single presumptive risk indicator.

Event-Based Models: The RMS Terrorism Risk Model

Event-based models are built upon relatively detailed analysis of con-sequences from specific attack scenarios. These models include sensi-tivity analysis for important parameters that affect consequences. They may include components to model multiple types of events and multiple targets. They may also include modules that translate expert judgments of likelihood or consequences. The strength of event-based models lies in the greater detail they enable in analysis. The weakness is that to obtain this detail analysts must estimate many uncertain pa-rameters that define the attack scenarios. One example of an event-based model is the RMS Terrorism Risk Model. The RMS model was developed as a tool for the insurance and reinsurance industries to assess risks of macroterrorism.

To reflect risk as a function of threat, vulnerability, and conse-quences, the RMS model calculates the expected annual consequences (human and economic) from diverse terrorist threats. The methodol-ogy relies on models of specific threat scenarios, calculations of eco-nomic and human life consequences of each scenario, and assessments of the relative probability of different types of attacks on different tar-gets. The RMS model calculates the threat of different types of at-tacks at different targets using expert judgment about target selection by terrorists, capabilities for different attack modes, overall likelihood of attack, and propensity to stage multiple coordinated attacks.

The RMS model assesses vulnerability by taking into account how security measures may lower the overall level of threat to a class of targets or deflect risk from one target to another. It then calculates the consequences of terrorist attacks for 37 attack modes (see Table 4.2) viewed as representative of the types of events that terrorists are capable of and motivated to attempt. Consequences are assessed in terms of economic losses, injuries, and fatalities using geocoded databases of population density, human activity patterns, business activities, and values of buildings and their contents.

RMS selected the attack modes to be sufficiently distinct and well enough defined so that it is possible to specify scenario parame-

Table 4.2
Modes of Attack Modeled in the RMS Terrorism Risk Model

Attack Mode	Description and Alternatives
Surface-to-air missile	Commercial jet airliner shot down
Bomb	600-lb; one-ton; two-ton; five-ton; or 10-ton
Aircraft impact	Hijacked commercial jet airliner flown into a target
Conflagration	9,000-gallon gasoline tanker hijacked and set on fire
Sabotage: industrial, explosion	5-, 50-, or 150-ton trinitrotoluene (TNT) equivalent
Sabotage: industrial, toxic release	5%, 40%, or 100% of Bhopal accident
Sabotage: industrial, explosion + release	5-ton + 5% Bhopal; 50-ton + 40% Bhopal; or 150-ton + 100% Bhopal
Sabotage: nuclear plant, radiation release	0.5%; 5%; or 20% of inventory
Dirty bomb, cesium 137	1,500 Curies or 15,000 Curies
Chemical, sarin gas	Indoors: 10 kg; Outdoors: 10 kg; 300 kg; or 1,000 kg
2% anthrax slurry released outdoors	1 kg, 10 kg, or 75 kg of slurry
Weaponized anthrax released indoors	40 g of weaponized anthrax
Smallpox	10, 100, or 1,000 initially infected
Genetically engineered smallpox	100 or 1,000 initially infected
Nuclear bomb	1 kiloton or 5 kiloton

SOURCE: RMS, Inc.

ters so that the losses from the event can be modeled. Sensitivity analysis is used to estimate the expected event outcomes given a range of relevant model parameters for each event scenario. For example, models using plume dispersion estimates take account of variation in wind speed, release point above ground, and atmospheric stability. However, the events were also selected to represent a sufficiently wide range of potential attacks to cover the loss potential from terrorism. While some may view this list to be comprehensive, others may notice that attacks involving suicide bombers, liquefied natural gas (LNG) tankers, or other commonly discussed attack modes have been omitted. This point identifies an important limitation of event-based models. That is, results are dependent on a large number of underlying assumptions.

The RMS Terrorism Risk Model allows analysts to test the robustness of model results to assumptions through parametric analysis of threat, vulnerability, and consequences. One way this is done is through use of elicited threat outlooks. The expert elicitation process used by RMS has produced three perspectives on terrorist threat for the next year: a standard, enhanced, and reduced threat outlook. All of these perspectives incorporate consideration of al Qaeda and associated groups, other foreign threat groups including Hizballah, and domestic terrorist groups.[1] Each perspective represents an aggregation of different beliefs about terrorist motivations and capabilities.

Table 4.3 provides an overview of the assumptions used for each of the included threat perspectives. The standard outlook assumes a terrorist threat that is primarily from al Qaeda, though potentially from other foreign organizations, with al Qaeda having a low likelihood of using CBRN weapons, and an overall low likelihood of multiple, coordinated attacks. The enhanced outlook reflects a greater likelihood that a terrorist attack might occur, that al Qaeda might use CBRN attacks, and that attacks would involve multiple, coordinated events. The enhanced outlook also has a higher Threat Reduction

---

[1] Domestic terrorist groups considered include right-wing, left-wing, and special interest group extremists.

Table 4.3
How Terrorism Outlooks in the RMS Model Reflect Perspectives on Threat

RMS Risk Outlooks 2004	Probability of One or More Attacks (Al Qaeda/Other Foreign)	Probability of Chemical, Biological, Radiological, or Nuclear Terrorism (Al Qaeda/Other Foreign)	Multiplicity[a] (Al Qaeda/Other Foreign)	Threat Reduction Factor[b]
Standard	33% / 18%	10% / 0%	Low / Very Low	0.5
Enhanced Threat	40% / 18%	20% / 0%	Moderate / Very Low	0.6
Reduced Threat	33% / 0%	0% / 0%	Low / —	0.5

NOTES: (a) Adjusts relative probabilities of events based upon the probability that coordinated attacks take place. (b) Adjusts the relative probabilities given that security measures make subsequent attacks more difficult after a single event occurs in a given year.

Factor, reflecting that with a heightened awareness of terrorism activities, security measures would be tighter and have a greater effect on reduction of secondary attacks after a single attack happens. Finally, the reduced outlook assumes that the only macroterrorist threats to the United States are those posed by al Qaeda.

We used the RMS Terrorism Risk Model to calculate expected annual consequences of terrorist attacks (i.e., terrorism risk). Losses were expressed in terms of numbers of fatalities, numbers of injuries, and total property damage in dollars (buildings, building contents, and business interruption). Impacts were then aggregated across the urban areas that received funding through the UASI grant program by summing the expected annual consequences for each of the attack-mode target pairs modeled for an urban area.

Calculating an Aggregated Risk Estimator

By considering three perspectives on threat (the RMS standard, enhanced, and reduced threat outlooks), the RMS results provide three perspectives on terrorism risk for the UASI-funded urban areas. Results from the RMS model are shown in Table 4.4. Though 50 urban

Table 4.4
Estimates of Expected Annual Terrorism Consequences in UASI Urban Areas

Urban Areas	RMS Risk Outlook								
	Combined Property Total ($ million)			Fatalities			Total Injuries		
	Standard	Reduced	Increased	Standard	Reduced	Increased	Standard	Reduced	Increased
Albany-Schenectady-Troy	0.4	0.4	0.4	0.001	0.0004	0.001	0.03	0.01	0.04
Atlanta	2.3	1.7	3.1	1.4	0.8	2.0	24	14	36
Baltimore	2.4	1.3	3.2	0.6	0.1	1.5	14	3	28
Baton Rouge	0.2	0.2	0.2	0.0002	0	0.001	0.1	0	0.1
Boston, MA-NH	18	8.3	26	12	8	17	213	126	305
Buffalo-Niagara Falls	1.0	0.7	1.5	0.3	0.1	0.5	6	2	10
Charlotte-Gastonia-Rock Hill, NC-SC	1.1	0.6	1.4	0.1	0.03	0.2	4	0.8	6
Chicago	115	77	150	54	38	73	1,158	820	1,513
Cincinnati, OH-KY-IN	0.9	0.8	1.1	0.1	0.0	0.2	1.8	0.8	3.3
Cleveland-Lorain-Elyria	3.0	1.4	4.3	0.5	0.1	1.0	15	3	26
Columbus, OH	0.7	0.6	0.8	0.05	0.01	0.1	1.1	0.3	2
Dallas	2.1	1.4	3.0	1.5	0.9	2.3	27	16	42
Denver	2.5	1.8	3.3	1.1	0.7	1.6	19	11	28
Detroit	4.2	2.1	5.7	1.9	0.9	3.1	42	20	66
Fresno	0.2	0.2	0.2	0.0003	0	0.001	0.001	0	0.002
Houston	11	6.7	15	9	6	12	151	98	213

Table 4.4—continued

Urban Areas	RMS Risk Outlook								
	Combined Property Total ($ million)			Fatalities			Total Injuries		
	Standard	Reduced	Increased	Standard	Reduced	Increased	Standard	Reduced	Increased
Indianapolis	0.7	0.6	0.8	0.1	0.02	0.1	1.3	0.5	2.6
Jersey City	4.4	0.2	9.1	2	0.004	5	50	0.2	115
Kansas City, MO-KS	1.1	1.0	1.2	0.05	0.01	0.1	1.1	0.4	2
Las Vegas, NV-AZ	4.1	2.8	5.9	1	0.4	2	24	10	45
Los Angeles-Long Beach[a]	34	16	58	17	7	31	385	144	716
Louisville, KY-IN	0.6	0.6	0.6	0.0004	0	0.001	0	0	0
Memphis, TN-AR-MS	0.5	0.5	0.5	0.0004	0	0.001	0	0	0
Miami, FL	2.7	1.3	3.9	0.5	0.4	0.7	9	6	12
Milwaukee-Waukesha, WI	1.1	0.6	1.3	0.1	0.02	0.1	3	0.4	5
Minneapolis-St. Paul, MN-WI[b]	2.7	2.0	3.4	0.4	0.1	0.8	10	4	19
New Haven-Meriden, CT	1.1	0.4	1.2	0.02	0.0001	0.04	2	0.004	4
New Orleans	0.8	0.6	0.9	0.1	0.01	0.1	2	0.4	3
New York, NY	413	265	550	304	221	401	5,046	3,322	6,864
Newark, NJ	7.3	0.8	12	4	0.1	9	70	2	153
Oakland, CA	4.0	1.1	8.4	1	0.03	3	25	1	63
Orange County, CA[c]	3.7	1.0	6.7	2	0.01	6	41	0.5	97
Orlando	0.6	0.4	0.9	0.1	0.03	0.3	3	1	7
Philadelphia, PA-NJ	21	8	28	9	5	13	190	92	273

Table 4.4—continued

Urban Areas	Combined Property Total ($ million)			RMS Risk Outlook Fatalities			Total Injuries		
	Standard	Reduced	Increased	Standard	Reduced	Increased	Standard	Reduced	Increased
Phoenix-Mesa	1.9	1.6	2.1	0.1	0.02	0.3	3	1	6
Pittsburgh	1.0	0.8	1.3	0.1	0.01	0.1	2	0.5	3
Portland-Vancouver, OR-WA	2.0	1.9	2.2	0.1	0.03	0.2	2	1	4
Richmond-Petersburg	0.4	0.4	0.4	0.001	0.0004	0.001	0.1	0.02	0.1
Sacramento	0.7	0.6	0.8	0.1	0.02	0.2	2	1	3
St. Louis, MO-IL	2.1	1.6	2.8	0.6	0.3	1.0	12	7	20
San Antonio	0.4	0.3	0.5	0.05	0.01	0.1	1	0.3	2
San Diego	2.8	1.4	4.4	1	0.4	2	28	12	47
San Francisco	57	38	81	24	16	36	448	300	643
San Jose	1.7	1.0	2.8	0.4	0.1	1	9	2	20
Seattle-Bellevue-Everett	6.7	4.4	10	4	3	6	84	52	126
Tampa-St. Petersburg-Clearwater	0.9	0.6	1.4	1	0.2	1	10	4	18
Washington, DC-MD-VA-WV	36	21	59	29	16	48	652	405	1,014

NOTE: (a) Los Angeles and Long Beach received separate UASI disbursements though are considered together in this analysis. (b) Minneapolis and St. Paul received separate UASI disbursements though are considered together in this analysis. (c) Santa Ana and Anaheim received separate UASI disbursements though are considered together in this analysis as Orange County.

areas were allocated UASI funding in FY2004, several of these were analyzed as larger urban areas because of how the RMS model is configured. Specifically, Los Angeles and Long Beach, Santa Ana and Anaheim, and Minneapolis and St. Paul received separate allocations but were modeled as Los Angeles-Long Beach, Orange County, and Minneapolis-St. Paul, respectively. As a result, the analysis covers 47 urban areas instead of 50. Subsequent discussions only use risk estimates derived from expected fatalities. However, the data in this table indicates that for results from the RMS model, expected fatalities, injuries, and economic losses are highly correlated with each other.

For the purpose of estimating each region's overall risk, we must select a single risk estimate for each city. Moreover, we would like the overall risk estimate to characterize risk well, regardless of which of the three threat perspectives proves to be closest to true risk. As discussed in Chapter Three, doing so requires combining multiple estimates of terrorism risk. We calculated an aggregated risk estimator from the three sets of expected fatalities generated by the RMS model, c_{ij},[1] using a constrained optimization. The optimization identified a set of nonnegative city shares of total risk, r_i, that sum to one, and minimize the objective function,

$$\sum_{i=1}^{47} \sum_{j=1}^{3} I_{ij} (c_{ij} - r_i)^2$$

where I_{ij} is an indicator variable taking the value 1 if $c_{ij} > r_i$ (i.e., risk is underestimated) or else the value 0. This functional form of objective function used in this analysis incorporates several assumptions.

First, the objective function above minimizes underestimation error as opposed to overall error. This is based on our judgment that is better to minimize potential losses from terrorism that could result from underestimating risk than it is to ensure that each city has an equal chance of having its risk over- or underestimated. This assumption tends to favor regions that have a distribution of consequences

---

[1] i designates the urban area and j designates the threat estimate used.

with a tail representing very large consequences. Thus, risk estimates for dense, urban areas will be larger using this approach than an ordinary sum of squares minimization. Increasing estimates for cities like New York means that the larger cities to do not bear a disproportionate share of potential risk underestimation. Another reasonable approach would be to minimize overall sum of squares with an objective function that set I_{ij} in the equation above to a constant value of 1. While this objective function is better understood mathematically, it is not more desirable normatively. The subsequent analysis only presents results using the objective function minimizing underestimation error. Analysis using an overall error objective function leads to qualitatively similar, though not identical results.

Second, using squared error assumes that larger errors are much worse than smaller errors. If underestimation error is linked to preventable fatalities or other damages, this assumption reflects realities about risk perceptions of catastrophic events.

Finally, this analysis only accounts for risk as measured by expected fatalities. As discussed previously, a complete treatment of terrorism risk estimation must use methods from the literatures on multiobjective decisionmaking to provide transparency into value judgments regarding balancing across different types of consequences.

Comparison of Population, Density-Weighted Population, and the Aggregated Estimate of Urban Area Risk Shares

Figure 4.1 compares estimates of urban area shares of risk derived from our aggregated estimator, and two commonly used indicators, population and density-weighted population. For comparison, the shares of DHS FY2004 UASI allocations are also included in this figure, along with a vertical line representing equal shares across all funded urban areas. A table listing the data in Figure 4.1 can be found in Appendix A.

Shares of total population across the UASI-funded urban areas are presented as filled circles. The size of city shares of risk using this

Figure 4.1
City Shares of Total Risk Estimated Using Four Indicators of Risk, Sorted by Aggregated Estimate, with a Vertical Line Indicating Equal Risk Across Cities

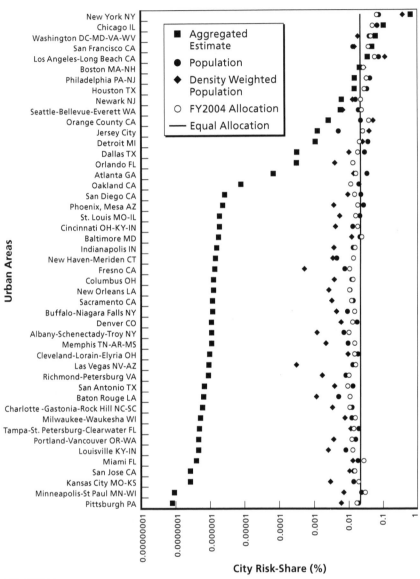

measure ranges from a high of 0.076 of total risk (Los Angeles-Long Beach, CA) to a low of 0.004 (New Haven-Meriden, CT), with 14 metropolitan areas having shares greater than the equal-share line.

Density-weighted population shares (filled squares in Figure 4.1) run from a high of 0.378 (New York) to 0.0003 (Las Vegas), thus resulting in a much larger spread of estimated shares of total risk than derived by the population estimator. Moreover, using density-weighted population, just eight cities are found to have more than the equal-share allocation of terrorism risk.

The aggregated estimates of city risk-shares are displayed in Figure 4.1 as open diamonds. Immediately apparent is that most of these estimates of city risk shares are several orders of magnitude lower than the population or density-weighted population estimates. The aggregated estimates range from 7.87E-8 (Pittsburgh) to 0.672 (New York), with just six cities having shares greater than the equal share. Interestingly, by more equally distributing underestimation risk, the aggregated estimator causes 32 of the UASI urban areas to be counted as having virtually no share of total terrorism risk. If, for instance, the $675 million FY04 UASI funds had been distributed in proportion to the aggregate estimate of city risk, these cities would have received less than $70,000 in total.

Most of the concentration in risk found with the aggregated estimator is due to similar concentrations in the RMS estimates of expected annual terrorism consequences for each metropolitan area. Across threat outlooks, New York has an average of 58 percent of total expected losses in the RMS model, and six of the metropolitan areas account for more than 95 percent of total losses. Clearly, the aggregated estimator is sensitive to this underlying model of terrorism risk.

Alternatively, other terrorism risk models that reflect threat and vulnerability information not captured in the RMS model would be expected to yield an aggregated estimator that suggests less concentration of risk, if the model estimates were similarly less concentrated.

Finally, Figure 4.1 shows how FY2004 UASI allocations (open circles) compare with risk estimates. Shares of UASI funding closely track urban areas' shares of population. On average, city population shares differ from grant allocation shares by just 0.006, with the maximum discrepancy of 0.02 occurring for Los Angeles. If one believes the underlying assumptions of the RMS Terrorism Risk Model, then the distribution of resources does not match the distribution of terrorism risk. As stated previously, this might be acceptable because of issues of cost effectiveness of available risk reduction opportunities.

CHAPTER FIVE

Evaluating the Performance of Different Estimates of Terrorism Risk

We have argued that uncertainties in the distribution of terrorism risk necessitate risk estimates that perform well across a range of assumptions about terrorist threat, vulnerability, and consequences. In this chapter, we describe a model for evaluating the performance of alternative risk estimates across a range of plausible terrorism futures. We use this model to compare the robustness to uncertainty of three estimates introduced earlier: the population, density-weighted population, and the proposed aggregated estimate as indicators of the share of terrorism risk for each of the UASI urban areas.

The Performance of Terrorism Risk Estimates

The population, density-weighted population, and aggregated estimates each offer a different solution to the problem of estimating cities' unobservable share of true risk, from here forward referred to as a city's risk share. Given these differences, it is important to know which indicator offers the most robust depiction of true risk. As we discussed previously, however, we are less concerned with the problem of indicators overestimating true risk than we are with underestimation of true risk; therefore, we define an estimator's performance in terms of how well it minimizes underestimation of each urban area's terrorism risk share.

Since true risk shares are not directly observable, we conduct a series of simulations to explore the performance of the estimators across a range of plausible values for each city's true risk share. We begin with a best-available estimate of urban areas' true risk shares, and then systematically allow simulated true risk to vary around these best estimates, examining how each of the risk-share estimators performs. In this way, we examine how robust the different estimators are to a wide range of plausible futures designed to represent uncertainties in terrorist motives, targets, methods, and capabilities that are fundamental to the description of cities' true risk shares.

Two sets of simulations were conducted. In the first, we took RMS estimates of expected annual consequences for each city as the best available estimate of true risk, and then systematically allow for the possibility that true risk may differ from the RMS estimates by up to two orders of magnitude. Thus, for instance, if the RMS estimate of expected annual terrorism fatalities for New York City is 304, we examine the performance of the estimators if true fatality risk for New York ranges from 3.04 to 30,400. Other urban areas' true risk shares were simultaneously, and independently, allowed to fluctuate around their RMS risk estimates by up to two orders of magnitude.

Because our aggregated estimator is derived from the same RMS estimates of city risk, this first simulation may lead to results biased in its favor. To address this limitation, we conducted a second simulation in which each estimator's performance was examined after assuming that cities' shares of true risk may vary by up to two orders of magnitude around their shares of total density-weighted population.

Simulation Methods

The simulations are designed to explore a range of possible values for true city risk shares, which values are then used to evaluate the performance of the city risk-share estimators. Each simulated true risk trial is constructed by assuming that the 47 urban areas, i, to have a set of true risk values, A_{ij}, for $j = 1,2, \ldots J$ types of risk, that randomly differ from some best estimates of that city's risk, E_{ij}, by up to a factor of k:

$$A_{ij} = E_{ij}k^u$$

where u is drawn from the uniform random distribution $U[-1,1]$. Thus, simulated true risk may range from E_{ij} / k to $E_{ij}k$, with roughly half of all simulations falling above or below a city's best risk estimate, E.

Simulated true absolute risk values for each type of risk, A_{ij}, are converted to true risk shares, R, by dividing each by the sum of all absolute true risk:

$$R_{ij} = \frac{A_{ij}}{\sum\limits_{i=1}^{47} A_{ij}}$$

In the first series of simulations, best estimates of true absolute risk (E) are derived from the RMS estimates of expected city consequences (injuries, fatalities, and property loss) across risk outlooks (standard, enhanced, and reduced risk), specifically:

- In Model 1a, "All Consequences, All Outlooks," three types of absolute risk are averaged to construct the simulated true risk shares (i.e., $J = 3$). These consist of the RMS estimates for expected city fatalities, injuries, and property loss across the three risk outlooks.
- In Model 1b, "All Consequences, Standard Outlook," the $J = 3$ types of absolute risk averaged to construct simulated true risk shares are the RMS estimates of expected city fatalities, injuries, and property loss for the standard risk outlook.
- In Model 1c, "All Consequences, Enhanced Outlook," the $J = 3$ types of absolute risk averaged to construct simulated true risk shares are the RMS estimates of expected city fatalities, injuries, and property loss for the enhanced risk outlook.
- In Model 1d, "All Consequences, Reduced Outlook," the $J = 3$ types of absolute risk averaged to construct simulated true risk shares are the RMS estimates of expected city fatalities, injuries, and property loss for the reduced risk outlook.

- In Model 1e, "Fatalities, All Outlooks," the J = 3 types of absolute risk averaged to construct simulated true risk shares are the RMS estimates of expected city fatalities under the three risk outlooks.
- In Model 1f, "Injuries, All Outlooks," the J = 3 types of absolute risk averaged to construct simulated true risk shares are the RMS estimates of expected city injuries under the three risk outlooks.
- In Model 1g, "Property Loss, All Outlooks," the J = 3 types of absolute risk averaged to construct simulated true risk shares are the RMS estimates of expected city fatalities under the three risk outlooks.

In Model 2, density-weighted population is used as the absolute risk estimate, E, to construct simulated true risk shares.

In all models, 5,000 trials are evaluated for each of seven values of k, the factor by which true risk is allowed to deviate from estimated absolute risk (k=1, 5, 10, 25, 50, 75, and 100). At k=1, simulated true risk shares are equal to the best estimates of true risk shares, whereas at k=100 simulated true risk shares deviate from the estimated true risk shares by up to a factor of 100.

The performance of each of the risk-share estimators, m, is evaluated for each set of simulated true risk shares by examining the sum of squared underestimation error across cities:

$$P_m = \sum_{j=1}^{J} \sum_{i=1}^{47} I_{ij}(R_{ij} - U_{mi})^2$$

where I_{ij} is an indicator variable taking the value 1 if $R_{ij} > U_{mi}$, or else the value 0, and U_{mi} is the risk-share estimate for city i made by risk-share estimator m. Across simulations, we also examine the largest such sum of squared error to establish the worst case performance of each risk-share estimator at each value of k.

In addition to examining the performance of the three city risk-share estimators for each of the two surrogates for true risk, we include a sixth estimator for comparison purposes. This random risk-share estimator is recalculated in each simulation trial, and estimates each city's risk share as a random value drawn from a uniform distribution, $U[0,1]$, divided by the sum of the uniform values drawn for all cities in the current trial.

Simulation Results

Variability in city shares of overall risk. The simulations are designed to construct a range of plausible values for each of the UASI urban areas' shares of total terrorism risk, so that the robustness to different possible futures of the risk-share estimators can be compared. To illustrate the extent of variability in true city risk shares produced by the simulation, we examined maximum, minimum, and quartile risk shares for each city across the 5,000 simulation trials in Model 1a when true risk was allowed to vary from the RMS estimate of risk by one order of magnitude ($k = 10$). For this case, when true risk differs from the RMS estimates by up to one order of magnitude, share of total true risk for New York ranges from a minimum of 0.028 to a maximum of 0.961 of all UASI urban areas' total risk. Baton Rouge, in contrast, had a minimum true risk share of 0.000002, and a maximum of 0.0027 of all cities' risk. Similar variability in simulated true risk-shares was observed in each of the models. These results are shown in Figure 5.1, where the share of total true risk across the $J = 3$ risk types for city i is calculated as follows:

$$\frac{\sum_{j=1}^{J} R_{ij}}{\sum_{i=1}^{47} \sum_{j=1}^{J} R_{ij}} = \frac{\sum_{j=1}^{J} R_{ij}}{J}.$$

Figure 5.1
Simulation Results: Distribution of City Share of Total True Risk When True
Risk Deviates from RMS Estimates by up to a Factor of 10, Model 1a

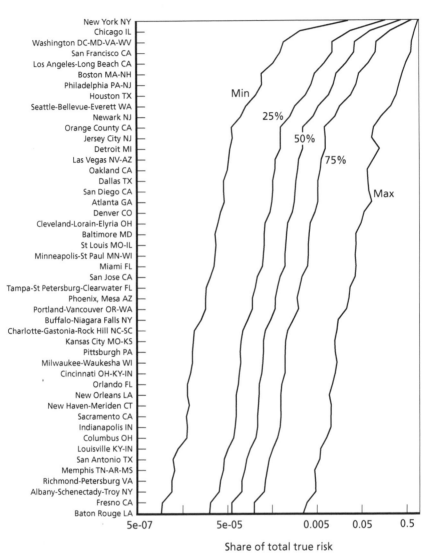

In the first series of models, simulated true risk varies around the RMS model estimates of expected fatalities, injuries, and property loss across terrorism risk outlooks. As such, these models use all or a superset of the RMS model estimates of risk as the basis for simulating true risk (three types of consequences in each of three terrorism risk outlooks). Since the aggregated estimator was developed to minimize underestimation error using the RMS model, it might be expected to outperform the other estimators. Nevertheless, we include measurements of the performance of the aggregated estimator in the first series of models, because it provides information on how well an optimized risk-share estimator could perform, which aids in the interpretation of the performance of the other risk-share estimators.

Figure 5.2 presents the mean underestimation error performance for the three risk-share estimators and the random estimator when true risk is assumed to vary around all nine RMS estimates of city terrorism risk (Model 1a). As expected, the random estimator is associated with the greatest underestimation error and the aggregated estimator is associated with the lowest underestimation error.

Figure 5.2
Mean Risk Underestimation as True Risk Deviates from Estimates: Model 1a

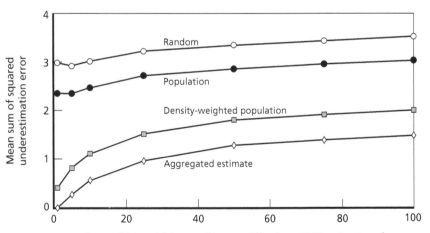

Interestingly, at all levels of k, the density-weighted population estimator resulted in underestimation error closer to that of the aggregated estimator than to that of the random or population estimators. The population estimator, in turn, had underestimation error that was consistently closer to that of the random estimator than to that of either the density-weighted population or robust estimators.

As noted earlier, the simulation procedures allowed for considerable variability in simulated true risk estimates. For instance, in some trials New York accounted for less than one percent of total risk, whereas in others it accounted for more than 99 percent. Given this degree of uncertainty, it is useful to examine worst-case scenarios for the various city risk-share estimators.

Figure 5.3 presents the maximum underestimation error observed across 5,000 simulations for each of the risk-share estimators as the variability of the simulated true risk increases. In this worst-case analysis, the estimators exhibit the same rank ordering as found with mean underestimation error, with the random estimator performing most poorly and the aggregated estimator performing best. However, the maximum underestimation error increases only modestly for $k > 30$.

Figures A.1 through A.3, in Appendix A, describe estimator performance when simulated true risk is based on just the RMS standard, enhanced, or reduced terrorism threat outlooks (Models 1b, 1c, and 1d). Figures A.4 through A.6, in Appendix A, describe estimator performance when just fatalities, injuries, or property loss are considered as the basis for simulating different true risk scenarios. These models test the performance of the risk-share estimators across alternative value judgments about what types of consequences are of greatest concern. Each of these models uses just a subset of the data used to calculate the robust estimator, and again it outperforms all other city risk-share estimators. Indeed, the relative performance of the risk-share estimators in each of these models is similar to that found in Model 1a.

Figure 5.3
**Maximum Risk Underestimation as True Risk Deviates from Estimates:
Model 1a**

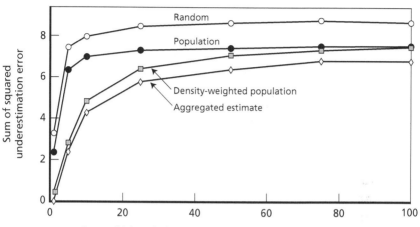

Factor (k) by which true risk may differ from RMS estimates of
risk combining all threat outlooks and all consequences

In Model 2, simulated true risk is based on density-weighted population, rather than RMS estimates of risk. As seen in Figure 5.4, this change has the effect of making the density-weighted population estimator the optimal choice, at least when true risk is assumed to differ from density-weighted populations by no more than a factor of five. Interestingly, however, the aggregated estimator exhibits a comparable mean underestimation error to the density-weighted population estimator for higher levels of k. As in the first series of models, the population estimator produces underestimation errors closer to the random estimator than to either the density-weighted population estimator or the aggregated estimator.

Figure 5.5 presents the worst-case performances for Model 2. Here the aggregated estimator clearly exhibits higher underestimation error than the density-weighted population estimator, but otherwise the relative performance of the estimators is similar to what has been observed in all earlier models.

Figure 5.4
Mean Risk Underestimation as True Risk Deviates from Estimates: Model 2

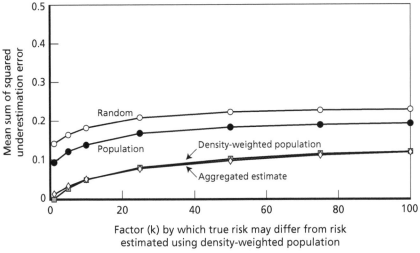

Figure 5.5
Maximum Risk Underestimation as True Risk Deviates from Estimates:
Model 2

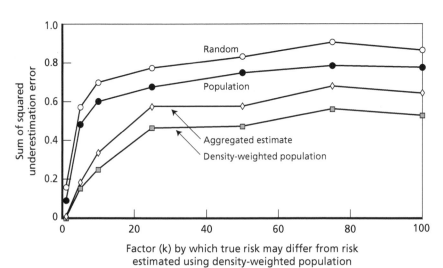

Discussion of simulation results. The consistency of findings across the models has several important implications. First, the aggregated estimator exhibits as low or lower mean underestimation error than all other estimators considered in this study. As discussed previously, this was expected in the first series of models in which the same data used to generate the robust estimator were used to simulate true city risk. Nevertheless, given that we cannot directly observe true risk, we must estimate relative risk based on some best-available model of city risk. Our models show that using procedures like those we developed to produce the aggregated estimator, a one-dimensional estimator can be calculated that minimizes mean underestimation error across multidimensional model-based risk information, and which therefore exhibits lower mean underestimation error given uncertainties than alternative estimates of city risk shares. Similarly, even when worst-case scenarios are sought, defined as those simulated allocations of true city risk that maximize estimator error, the aggregated estimator exhibits lower underestimation error than all other estimators, or, in the case of Model 2, performed nearly as well as the best estimator.

Second, the density-weighted population estimator results in substantially reduced underestimation error in comparison to the random and population estimators. Moreover, in the first series of models, it performed nearly as well as the aggregated estimator, and in the second model, it was equivalent to or better than the aggregated estimator. The good performance of the density-weighted population estimator makes it particularly attractive for problems of establishing terrorism risk shares when sophisticated models of risk are unavailable or when there is a need for a simple and transparent risk model, as might be the case should such models need to be publicly debated.

Third, across all the trials, allocating resources using the population-based approach fares little better than the random estimator that treats Baton Rouge as having a share of risk equivalent to New York—or flipping a coin. The random estimator consistently performed worse than all other estimators, but perhaps not as differently as might be expected. This equal distribution of risk shares led to performance not far worse than the performance of the population-based approach. This finding raises important questions about the appropriateness of population as a risk indicator.

Finally, the aggregated risk estimator's performance on different unidimensional risk perspectives is a measure of its robustness. In this study, the relative utility of the different city risk-share estimators does not depend strongly on whether or not terrorists are likely to employ weapons of mass destruction. That is, when we base our simulation on true risk estimates that assume terrorists will not use weapons of mass destruction (the RMS Reduced terrorism outlook) in Model 1d, we find essentially the same pattern of estimator performance as when we base the simulation on estimates of relative city risk that assume that the risk of a WMD attack is even greater than suggested by current conventional wisdom (the RMS Enhanced terrorism outlook). We find a similar invariance in estimator performance across consequence types (fatalities, injuries, and property loss). For the models used in this study, the aggregated estimator is relatively robust to fluctuations in the likelihood of WMD attacks and assumptions that prioritize lives or property. In the discussion that follows, these observations are dependent upon the models used in this study and may differ if other models are considered. However, the approach used to assess robustness would remain valid.

To summarize, the aggregated estimator performed well relative to other estimators, providing a proof of concept that a single, one-dimensional estimate of city risk shares can offer a solution to the problem of determining cities' relative risks that can be robust to uncertainties about the likelihood of WMD attacks, uncertainties about which consequences ought to be prioritized, and uncertainties about the expected magnitude of risks each city might face. Furthermore, the density-weighted population estimator fared better than the other simple estimators and even outperformed the aggregated estimator in some cases.

Limitations of the modeling exercise. The findings in this chapter are subject to a number of model limitations, several of which we now consider.

Clearly, the first series of models reported here depend on the assumption that the RMS estimates offer reasonably good approximations of the distribution of true terrorism risk across the 47 urban areas. Different assumptions about the distribution of true risk could lead to different conclusions about the performance of the different estimators. For instance, the RMS model describes terrorism risk largely as a threat to urban areas. Models that provide more detail into threats to rural areas, such as agroterrorism, would likely provide different observations. However, they, too, could easily be incorporated into the methodology demonstrated in this study. By rerunning the model assuming that true risk is distributed proportionally to density-weighted population (Model 2), we were able to offer a limited test of the sensitivity of our results to our reliance on RMS estimates. This tests a case where true risk is more accurately reflected with a simple model rather than a complex model like RMS. A more complete test would compare estimator performance when true risk is simulated using an independent event-based model of city risk.

Our approach to simulating uncertainty in true risk shares and estimator performance relies on assumptions that may be incorrect or inadequate. In simulating true city risk shares, for instance, we alter each city's RMS risk estimate by a factor k^u, where u is a random variable with a uniform [-1,1] distribution. This approach ensured that approximately half of all trials would have simulated true risk values lower than the RMS estimates, and half would have larger values. But alternative distributions for the random variable and alternative approaches to modeling variation in true risk are possible and might lead to different conclusions.

To explore the sensitivity of our results to assumptions about the distribution of u we reran Models 1a through 1g using a range of alternative distributions for u, including a U-shaped symmetric distribution (in which u was drawn from a Beta distribution with alpha=0.2, beta=0.2 and which ranged from –1 to 1, $B[0.2,0.2;-1,1]$), an inverse U-shaped symmetric distribution ($B[10,10,-1,1]$), and asymmetric distributions skewed toward –1 or 1, ($B[0.2,5,-1,1]$ and $B[5,0.2,-1,1]$). In each of these model series, the relative performance of the risk-share estimators for both mean underestimation error and maximum underestimation error was identical to those reported above when using a uniform distribution for u.

Another modeling assumption we made was that the harms associated with underestimating city risk shares are not linearly related to the magnitude of the underestimation but rather grow exponentially with underestimation errors. As such, we measured estimator performance by summing the square of underestimation error, rather than, for instance, the sum of underestimation errors or other aggregations of error. This decision treats a risk underestimation error of 0.2 for some city as substantially worse than underestimation by 0.1 at two cities, for example. Although this assumption appears reasonable, the true relationship between underestimation errors and harms may be different and not well described by squared error. A more complete test would compare estimator performance when error is assumed to be the absolute deviations instead of squared deviations.

CHAPTER SIX

Conclusions and Recommendations

To improve the allocation of homeland security resources and thereby to reduce loss of life and property to terrorism or minimize poor investments in homeland security measures if attacks do not take place, it is essential to have good estimates of the terrorism risk to which different regions or groups are exposed. This objective has been difficult to achieve for many reasons, including confusion about the definition of risk and the absence of a systematic framework for selecting risk indicators. This monograph offers a definition of risk and discusses the relationships among threats, vulnerabilities, consequences, and risk. In addition, it suggests a method for constructing a single-dimensional estimate of city risk shares, designed to perform well across a wide range of threat scenarios, risk types, and other sources of uncertainty. Finally, it proposes and demonstrates a framework for comparing the performance of alternative risk estimates given uncertainty in terrorists' intentions and capabilities, target vulnerabilities, and the likely consequences of successful terrorist attacks.

Defining Terrorism Risk

Estimating or measuring terrorism risk is incomplete without a framework that considers threat, vulnerability, and consequences. To establish a specific and actionable framework for analysis we develop definitions for threats as external, dynamic forces acting on targets or infrastructure and vulnerabilities as properties of the targets themselves. Together threat and vulnerability define the probability that specific types of damage-causing attacks will occur at specific targets during specified periods. The methods used to estimate threat are qualitatively different than those used to measure vulnerability and consequences. The former relies on collection and interpretation of intelligence. The latter requires scientific and engineering expertise of attack modes and target responses to attacks. Finally, threat, vulnerability, and consequences are interdependent since terrorism and homeland security is a multisided game, and terrorists may act strategically to increase their effectiveness. Thus, interactions between threat, vulnerability, and consequences have important consequences for risk management, though not explicitly discussed in these models.

Reflecting Uncertainty in Terrorism Risk Assessment

Effective assessment of terrorism risks requires measures that can accommodate the uncertainty inherent in the problem. We have proposed a method for estimating terrorism risk that hedges against uncertainties in threats, vulnerabilities, and consequences. Similar to practices used in economic forecasting, this estimator aggregates information from multiple models or experts. The aggregated estimator is robust in that it reflects a range of assumptions about terrorist threat and perspectives on relative importance of different measures of consequences. Further, we generate this aggregated estimator using an approach that minimizes the extent to which risk is underestimated across urban areas. Since aggregation can mask important differences between models or experts, it is important to consider how this aggregated estimate differs from estimates based on single perspectives.

Simple Versus Event-Based Risk Estimates

We describe and compare two approaches frequently used to estimate risk: simple indicators and event-based models. Examples of simple indicators include population and density-weighted population. The RMS Terrorism Risk Model is presented as an example of event-based models. We argue that event-based models offer a framework for calculating risk that overcomes some of the arbitrariness of simple indicators of risk that rely on presumptive correlate relationships.

Supporting this claim requires an approach to evaluation that accommodates several types of uncertainty. In Chapter Five, we demonstrated a simulation method for evaluating the relative performance of alternative risk estimates across plausible terrorism futures. This method provides insights into both distinctions between risk estimators and the variance of single estimators to assumptions about threat, vulnerability, and consequences.

This analysis showed that our aggregated estimator exhibited as low or lower underestimation error than risk estimates based on population and density-weighted population, demonstrating that a single estimate of city risk shares can offer a solution to the problem of determining cities' shares of total risk that is robust to a wide range of plausible terrorism risk futures.

The density-weighted population estimator results in substantially reduced underestimation error in comparison to the random and population estimators. In many cases, density-weighted population performs comparably to the robust estimator. This suggests that for some purposes, use of density-weighted population as a simple risk indicator might be preferred when, for example, they are informing decisions with a strategic time horizon and lead time.

Decisionmakers may wish to estimate risk to inform strategic resource allocations, operational resource allocations, or to evaluate how terrorism risk is changing. Strategic allocations differ from operational allocations in terms of the frequency and ease with which allocation decisions can be changed. Homeland security resources might be allocated strategically when they are expensive or infeasible to move or change once committed. For example, resources directed toward training emergency responders are constrained by the time it takes to complete training and the resistance of emergency response personnel to frequent relocation. On the other hand, operational allocations might be made in response to specific intelligence or to address short-term vulnerabilities. For example, the Democratic and Republican National Conventions in 2004 created new vulnerabilities, requiring enhanced security resources for a short period.

Density-weighted population is more appropriate than either population or random estimators for informing strategic resource allocations. The underlying data are easily obtained and provide credible, face-valid indicators of risk. Both of these factors increase the utility of density-weighted population in public debates about resource allocations.

Density-weighted population, however, does not allow decisionmakers to see how changes in threat or vulnerability information affect terrorism risk. For example, when making operational resource allocations or evaluating the effectiveness of preparedness programs, decisionmakers need to understand how specific countermeasures reduce or change the profile of terrorism risk. Similarly, a crude indicator like density-weighted population would offer no guidance about how city risk estimates might change with, for instance, new intelligence about terrorist targeting or capabilities of using WMD attacks. For these purposes, more detailed event-based models of terrorism risk are essential.

In this study, a single estimate was shown to be robust across uncertainties about the likelihood of WMD attacks, uncertainties about which consequences ought to be prioritized in considerations of city risk, and uncertainties about the expected magnitude of risks each city might face. For example, an important observation is that the risk profile of the 47 cities did not change significantly with the variability (or absence) of threats from weapons of mass destruction. While the primary focus of this study was not to estimate precisely terrorism risk in the United States, this observation raises questions about the distribution over many areas. In particular, one question might be to investigate whether risk is a characteristic a region's infrastructure or population that is relatively stable across different threats. If so, this would be an important observation when it comes to policy and resource decisions.

Observations about the variance of the aggregated risk estimate are dependent upon the results of the RMS model of terrorism risk and set of alternative estimates to which the aggregated estimate was compared. However, the proposed methods can be readily implemented with new data sources or other models. Adding new information to that provided by the RMS Terrorism Risk Model would presumably further improve the robust estimates.

Recommendations

The framework for defining terrorism risk and the analysis presented in this monograph, leads us to five recommendations for improving the allocation of homeland security resources.

1. DHS should consistently define terrorism risk in terms of expected annual consequences. Calculating expected annual consequences requires accounting for threat, vulnerability, and consequences. Defining terrorism risk in these terms facilitates the incorporation of risk reduction as the goal of homeland security programs.

2. DHS should seek robust risk estimators that account for uncertainty about terrorism risk and variance in citizen values. Given the tremendous uncertainties surrounding terrorism risk assessment, it is prudent to plan for the range of plausible futures that may play out. Several approaches are available for generating estimates of city risk shares that offer robust characterizations of risk across multiple uncertainties and perspectives on relative values of different consequences. Our approach to this problem ensures that underestimation error is minimized.

3. DHS should develop event-based models of terrorism risk, like that used by RAND and RMS. Measuring and tracking levels of terrorism risk is an important component of homeland security policy. These data provide insight into how current programs are reducing risk and when and where new terrorist threats may be emerging. Only event-based models of terrorism risk provide insight into how changes in assumptions or actual levels of threat, vulnerability, and consequences affect risk levels. This characteristic is important for informing operational level problems such as deciding which security and preparedness programs to implement. Furthermore, event-based models overcome a principal shortcoming of models that combine diverse risk indicators: They provide a coherent, defensible framework for selecting and combining information about threats, vulnerabilities, and consequences.

4. Until reliable event-based models are constructed, density-weighted population should be preferred over population as a simple risk indicator. Density-weighted population is reasonably correlated with the distribution of terrorism risk across the United States, as estimated by event-based models like the RMS Terrorism Risk Model. To support strategic policy decisions when the effects of new countermeasures or recent intelligence are not in question, density-weighted population is a useful indicator in lieu of event-based models. In contrast, our results suggest that population offers a remarkably weak indicator of risk, not much superior to estimating risk shares at random.

5. DHS should fund research to bridge the gap between terrorism risk assessment and resource allocation policies that are cost effective. Until the relationship between allocation amounts and risk reduction is understood, resource allocation decisions will not be optimized for reducing casualties and property loss. To these ends, DHS should evaluate the performance of the formula used to assign UASI grants using the approach presented in this study. Homeland security efforts will be greatly improved with better understanding of both the resources required to affect a range of countermeasures and the risk reduction achieved by affecting those countermeasures.

Supporting Figures and Table

Figure A.1
Mean Risk Underestimation as True Risk Deviates from Estimates: Model 1b

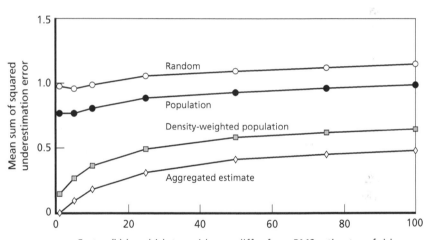

Factor (k) by which true risk may differ from RMS estimates of risk combining the RMS Standard threat outlook and all consequences

RAND *MG388-A.1*

Figure A.2
Mean Risk Underestimation as True Risk Deviates from Estimates: Model 1c

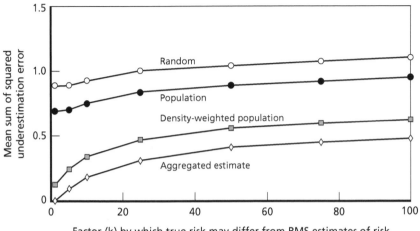

Factor (k) by which true risk may differ from RMS estimates of risk
combining the RMS Enhanced threat outlook and all consequences

Figure A.3
Mean Risk Underestimation as True Risk Deviates from Estimates: Model 1d

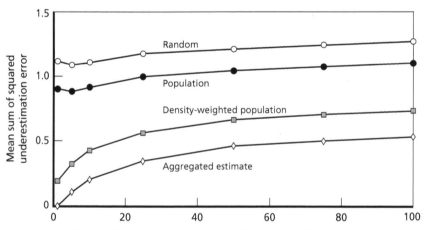

Factor (k) by which true risk may differ from RMS estimates of risk
combining the RMS Reduced threat outlook and all consequences

Figure A.4
Mean Risk Underestimation as True Risk Deviates from Estimates: Model 1e

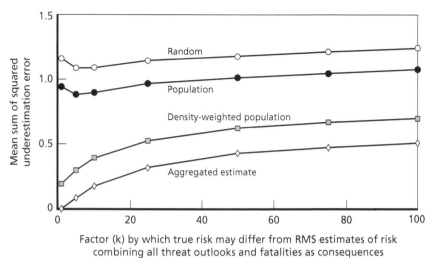

RAND *MG388-A.4*

Figure A.5
Mean Risk Underestimation as True Risk Deviates from Estimates: Model 1f

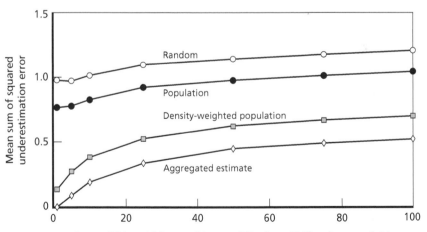

RAND *MG388-A.5*

Figure A.6
Mean Risk Underestimation as True Risk Deviates from Estimates: Model 1g

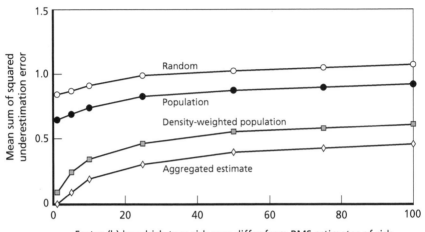

Factor (k) by which true risk may differ from RMS estimates of risk
combining all threat outlooks and property losses as consequences

Table A.1

Shares of 2003 DHS UASI and City Risk Shares Estimated Using Population, Density-Weighted Population, and Aggregated Estimator Methods

| Metro Area | DHS Allocation | Risk-Share Estimator | | |
		Population	Dens.-Wt. Pop.	Aggregated
Albany-Schenectady-Troy, NY	0.0102	0.0071	0.0012	1.08E-06
Atlanta, GA	0.0159	0.0335	0.0138	6.55E-05
Baltimore, MD	0.0236	0.0208	0.0124	1.69E-06
Baton Rouge, LA	0.0107	0.0049	0.0011	6.15E-07
Boston, MA-NH	0.0283	0.0278	0.0286	2.22E-02
Buffalo-Niagara Falls	0.0150	0.0095	0.0044	1.15E-06
Charlotte-Gastonia-Rock Hill, NC-SC	0.0110	0.0122	0.0033	5.71E-07
Chicago, IL	0.0506	0.0675	0.0673	1.10E-01
Cincinnati, OH-KY-IN	0.0189	0.0134	0.0040	1.82E-06
Cleveland-Lorain-Elyria, OH	0.0155	0.0184	0.0093	9.44E-07
Columbus, OH	0.0129	0.0126	0.0038	1.25E-06
Dallas, TX	0.0181	0.0287	0.0010	3.12E-04
Denver, CO	0.0128	0.0172	0.0059	1.10E-06
Detroit, MI	0.0204	0.0362	0.0252	1.04E-03
Fresno, CA	0.0105	0.0075	0.0005	1.33E-06
Houston, TX	0.0296	0.0341	0.0147	1.52E-02
Indianapolis, IN	0.0151	0.0131	0.0037	1.52E-06
Jersey City, NJ	0.0254	0.0050	0.0396	1.23E-03
Kansas City, MO-KS	0.0197	0.0145	0.0029	2.53E-07
Las Vegas, NV-AZ	0.0156	0.0128	0.0003	8.95E-07
Los Angeles-Long Beach	0.0599	0.0777	0.1111	3.73E-02
Louisville, KY-IN	0.0133	0.0084	0.0025	4.52E-07
Memphis, TN-AR-MS	0.0149	0.0093	0.0021	1.08E-06
Miami, FL	0.0284	0.0184	0.0130	3.95E-07
Milwaukee-Waukesha, WI	0.0151	0.0122	0.0077	5.23E-07

Table A.1—continued

| Metro Area | DHS Allocation | Risk-Share Estimator | | |
		Population	Dens.-Wt. Pop.	Aggregated
Minneapolis-St. Paul, MN-WI	0.0298	0.0242	0.0072	8.98E-08
New Haven-Meriden, CT	0.0143	0.0044	0.0034	1.39E-06
New Orleans, LA	0.0106	0.0109	0.0026	1.19E-06
New York, NY	0.0696	0.0760	0.3785	6.72E-01
Newark, NJ	0.0223	0.0166	0.0130	6.36E-03
Oakland, CA	0.0116	0.0195	0.0196	7.79E-06
Orange County, CA	0.0376	0.0232	0.0511	2.66E-03
Orlando, FL	0.0130	0.0134	0.0039	3.06E-04
Philadelphia, PA-NJ	0.0342	0.0416	0.0336	1.53E-02
Phoenix-Mesa, AZ	0.0181	0.0265	0.0036	2.27E-06
Pittsburgh, PA	0.0178	0.0192	0.0060	7.87E-08
Portland-Vancouver, OR-WA	0.0121	0.0156	0.0036	4.55E-07
Richmond-Petersburg, VA	0.0097	0.0081	0.0017	8.61E-07
Sacramento, CA	0.0119	0.0133	0.0032	1.18E-06
St. Louis, MO-IL	0.0160	0.0212	0.0053	1.84E-06
San Antonio, TX	0.0094	0.0130	0.0038	6.77E-07
San Diego, CA	0.0155	0.0230	0.0094	2.52E-06
San Francisco, CA	0.0392	0.0141	0.0147	4.78E-02
San Jose, CA	0.0148	0.0137	0.0109	2.67E-07
Seattle-Bellevue-Everett	0.0245	0.0197	0.0066	5.93E-03
Tampa-St. Petersburg-Clearwater, FL	0.0137	0.0195	0.0112	4.62E-07
Washington, DC-MD-VA-WV	0.0434	0.0402	0.0185	6.23E-02

Bibliography

Abt, Clark C., *The Economic Impact of Nuclear Terrorist Attacks on Freight Transport Systems in the Age of Seaport Vulnerability*, prepared for the U.S. Department of Transportation, Cambridge, Mass.: Abt Associates, 2003. Online at http://www.abtassociates.com/reports/ES-Economic_Impact_of_Nuclear_Terrorist_Attacks.pdf as of June 28, 2005.

Ayyub, Bilal M., *Risk Analysis for Critical Infrastructure and Key Asset Protection: Methods and Challenges*, presented at Symposium on Terrorism Risk Analysis, University of Southern California, Los Angeles, Calif., January 13–14, 2005. Online at http://www.usc.edu/dept/create/events/2004_11_18/Risk_Analysis_for_Critical_Infrastructure_and_Key_Asset_Protection.pdf as of June 28, 2005.

Bozzette, Samuel A., Rob Boer, Vibha Bhatnagar, Jennifer L. Brower, Emmett B. Keeler, Sally C. Morton, Michael A. Stoto, "A Model for a Smallpox-Vaccination Policy," *The New England Journal of Medicine*, Vol. 348, No. 5, 2003, pp. 416–425.

Canada, Ben, *State Homeland Security Grant Program: Hypothetical Distribution Patterns of a Risk-Based Formula*, Washington, D.C.: Congressional Research Service, 2003.

Chankong, Vira, and Yacov Y. Haimes, *Multiobjective Decisionmaking: Theory and Methodology*, New York: North Holland, 1983.

Clemen, Robert T., "Combining Economic Forecasts: A Review and Annotated Bibliography," *International Journal of Forecasting*, Vol. 5, No. 4, 1989, pp. 559–583.

DHS. See U.S. Department of Homeland Security.

Davis, Paul K., "Institutionalizing Planning for Adaptiveness," in Paul K. Davis, ed., *New Challenges for Defense Planning: Rethinking How Much Is Enough*, Santa Monica, Calif.: RAND Corporation, MR-400-RC, 1994, pp. 73–100. Online at http://www.rand.org/publications/MR/MR400 as of June 27, 2005.

Davis, Paul K., *Analytic Architecture for Capabilities-Based Planning, Mission-System Analysis, and Transformation*, Santa Monica, Calif.: RAND Corporation, MR-1513-OSD, 2002. Online at http://www.rand.org/publications/MR/MR1513 as of June 27, 2005.

Haimes, Yacov Y., *Risk Modeling, Assessment, and Management*, Hoboken, N.J.: Wiley-Interscience, 2004.

Hammond, John S., Ralph L. Keeney, and Howard Raiffa, *Smart Choices: A Practical Guide to Making Better Decisions*, Boston: Harvard Business School Press, 1999.

Howard, Ronald A., James E. Matheson, and Katherine L., *Readings in Decision Analysis*, 2nd ed., Menlo Park, Calif.: Decision Analysis Group, Stanford Research Institute, 1977.

Keeney, Ralph L., *Value-Focused Thinking: A Path to Creative Decisionmaking*, Cambridge, Mass.: Harvard University Press, 1992.

Keeney, Ralph L., and Howard Raiffa, *Decisions with Multiple Objectives: Preferences and Value Tradeoffs*, Cambridge, U.K.: Cambridge University Press, 1993.

Lakdawalla, Darius, and George Zanjani, *Insurance, Self-Protection, and the Economics of Terrorism*, Santa Monica, Calif.: RAND Corporation, 2004. Online at http://www.rand.org/publications/WR/WR171 as of June 28, 2005.

Lempert, Robert J., Steven W. Popper, and Steven C. Bankes, *Shaping the Next One Hundred Years: New Methods for Quantitative, Long-Term Policy Analysis*, Santa Monica, Calif.: RAND Corporation, MR-1626-CR, 2003. Online at http://www.rand.org/publications/MR/MR1626 as of June 27, 2005.

Morgan, M. Granger, Max Henrion, and Mitchell Small, *Uncertainty: A Guide to Dealing with Uncertainty in Quantitative Risk and Policy Analysis*, Cambridge: Cambridge University Press, 1990.

Morgan, M. Granger, and David W. Keith, "Subjective Judgments by Climate Experts," *Environmental Science and Technology*, Vol. 29, No. 10, 1995, pp. 468A–476A. Online at http://www.ucalgary.ca/~keith/papers/13.Morgan.1995.SubjectiveJudgmentsByClimate%20Experts.s.pdf as of July 16, 2005.

Paté-Cornell, M. Elizabeth, *Risks of Terrorist Attacks: Probabilistic Assessment and Use of Intelligence Information*, presented at Symposium on Terrorism Risk Analysis, University of Southern California, Los Angeles, Calif., January 15, 2005. Online at http://www.usc.edu/dept/create/events/2005_02_01/Risks_of_Terrorist_Attacks_Probabilistic_Assessment_and_use_of_Intelligence_Information.pdf as of June 28, 2005.

Ransdell, Tim, and Shervin Boloorian, *Federal Formula Grants and California*, Washington, D.C.: California Institute for Federal Policy Research, 2004.

Rinaldi, Steven M., James P. Peerenboom, and Terrence K. Kelly, "Identifying, Understanding, and Analyzing Critical Infrastructure Interdependencies," *IEEE Control Systems Magazine*, Vol. 21, No. 6, 2001, pp. 11–25.

Risk Management Solutions, *Managing Terrorism Risk*, Newark, Calif.: Risk Management Solutions, 2003. Online at http://www.rms.com/publications/terrorism_risk_modeling.pdf as of June 28, 2005.

RMS. See Risk Management Solutions.

Savage, L. J., "The Theory of Statistical Decision," *Journal of the American Statistical Association*, Vol 46, No. 253, 1951, pp. 55–67.

Stern, Paul C., and Harvey V. Fineberg, *Understanding Risk: Informing Decisions in a Democratic Society*, Washington, D.C.: National Academy Press, 1996.

U.S. Census Bureau, *United States Census 2000*, Washington, D.C.: U.S. Census Bureau, 2000. Online at http://www.census.gov/main/www/cen2000.html as of June 28, 2005.

U.S. Department of Homeland Security, Office for Domestic Preparedness, *Fiscal Year 2004 Urban Areas Security Initiative Grant Program: Program Guidelines and Application Kit*, Washington, D.C.: U.S. Department of Homeland Security, 2004. Online at http://www.dhs.gov/interweb/assetlibrary/grants_audit_fy04uasi.pdf as of June 27, 2005.

U.S. House of Representatives, Homeland Security: The Balance Between Crisis and Consequence Management Through Training and Assistance: Hearing Before the Subcommittee on Crime, Terrorism, and Homeland Security of the Committee on the Judiciary, Washington, D.C.: U.S. Government Printing Office, 2003. Online at http://frwebgate .access.gpo.gov/cgi-bin/getdoc.cgi?dbname=108_house_hearings&docid =f:90547.wais.pdf as of June 28, 2005.

von Winterfeldt, Detlof, and Heather Rosoff, *Using Project Risk Analysis to Counter Terrorism*, presented at Symposium on Terrorism Risk Analysis, University of Southern California, Los Angeles, Calif., January 13–14, 2005. Online at http://www.usc.edu/dept/create/events/2005_01_31/ Using_Project_Risk_Analysis_to_Counter_Terrorism.pdf as of June 28, 2005.

Woo, Gordon, *Quantifying Insurance Terrorism Risk*, Newark, Calif.: Risk Management Solutions, 2002a. Online at http://www.rms.com/ NewsPress/Quantifying_Insurance_Terrorism_Risk.pdf as of June 28, 2005.

———, *Understanding Terrorism Risk*, Newark, Calif.: Risk Management Solutions, 2002b. Online at http://www.rms.com/Publications/ UnderstandTerRisk_Woo_RiskReport04.pdf as of June 28, 2005.

Made in the USA
Lexington, KY
26 March 2018